Culinary temptations from

HOLLAND AMERICA LINE

HOLLAND AMERICA LINE

A Taste of
EXCELLENCE
COOKBOOK

VOLUME I
Culinary Signature Collection

RUDI SODAMIN

RIZZOLI
NEW YORK

First published in the United States of America in 2006 by
Rizzoli International Publications, Inc.
300 Park Avenue South
New York, NY 10010
www.rizzoliusa.com

© 2006 Holland America Line, Inc. and Rudi Sodamin

2006 2007 2008 2009 / 10 9 8 7 6 5 4 3 2 1

ISBN-13: 978-0-8478-2839-5
ISBN-10: 0-8478-2839-5

Library of Congress Control Number: 2006922887

Design: Susi Oberhelman

Printed in the United States

Photograph, page 1: Double Fudge Chocolate Avalanche Cake with Grand
Marnier Whipped Cream and Berry Sauce (recipe, page 169)
Photograph, page 2: Roasted Pheasant with Sweet Potato Purée, Sautéed
Cabbage, and Cranberry Compote (recipe, page 108)
Photograph, page 6: Trio of Crème Brûlées (recipe, page 161)

DEDICATION

This book is dedicated to those who expect excellence, and to those who provide it:

To the loyal guests of Holland America Line for the challenge your
sophisticated tastes and worldly knowledge present to our culinary team.

To all the tireless people who so beautifully orchestrate our intricate culinary programs—
those who seek out and purchase the superlative ingredients we use in the galley;
those who load provisions on the ships; those responsible for all the inventory and careful
storage; those who prepare the ingredients, create the recipes, cook the meals,
arrange our beautiful dining areas, serve the food, wash the china, keep our kitchens
gleaming, mix the drinks, and manage our storerooms, kitchens, dining rooms,
restaurants, and lounges; and to all the rest who bring their creativity,
talent, and hard work, quite literally, to the Holland America Line table.

CONTENTS

WELCOME

talent, technique, artistry, and aesthetic excellence of the painting itself, but also by the signature of the artist—say Van Gogh—which identifies the work as authentic, unique, and valuable. Masterful service and unparalleled accommodations are among the hallmarks of Holland America Line's Signature of Excellence.

In the distinguished history of the company, the Holland America Line guest experience has never been more exciting, interactive, and memorable. Our Signature of Excellence commitment provides you with elegant ships and accommodations; sophisticated five-star dining; gracious, unobtrusive service; extensive enrichment programs and activities; and compelling worldwide itineraries.

A key element in our success in bringing you the finest cuisine the maritime world has to offer is our partnership with Rudi Sodamin—the most highly decorated and celebrated master chef on the seven seas. Master Chef Rudi Sodamin is widely known for revolutionizing cuisine on cruise lines; his innovation and creativity have set the standard for our entire industry. Chef Sodamin is a master of details and a meticulous practitioner of what can best be described as high culinary art. When on one of our ships, take note of the excellence of our food preparation and the artistic presentation of each dish issued from our galleys. As Holland America Line's culinary consultant, Master Chef Rudi Sodamin is leading our culinary team to unprecedented heights of culinary excellence and providing exciting new concepts for enchanting and engaging our guests.

No less thrilling is our vessels' superlative environment; our commitment to providing five-star dining extends beyond the food itself and permeates every point of the Holland America Line culinary experience. Aboard our ships, you will notice our pursuit of perfection, which is reflected in the details: To step into one of our main dining rooms is to be transported to a breathtaking architectural wonder with sweeping ocean vistas, gracious service, and lovely fresh floral centerpieces. A meal in our award-winning Pinnacle Grill is an intimate experience in refinement from the elegance of our Frette® Linens, the ethereal lightness of our

Gracious service is a defining characteristic of our cruises. Every request—including two sugars with your tea—is happily accommodated.

A B O A R D !

Bvlgari® fine china, and the balance of our Riedel® stemware, the only crystal in the world expressly designed to enhance the experience of wine. Our industry-leading Lido restaurants hum with an unrivalled energy that defines this casual dining experience. Right down to our 24-hour complimentary room service, every detail of the look, feel, and taste of our meals is considered and delivered—right to your door.

Our team was truly excited when Master Chef Sodamin agreed to share some of his remarkable recipes for this project—our first volume of the *Holland America Line A Taste of Excellence Cookbook*. Included are unforgettable dishes hand-picked by Chef Sodamin from Holland America Line's extensive repertoire of Signature recipes, as well as photography showing how we present these dishes on board our ships. We hope this collection will inspire and delight you. And, on behalf of the fifteen thousand men and women of Holland America Line, we look forward to welcoming you aboard.

STEIN KRUSE
President and Chief Executive Officer

Stylish ships that offer incomparable sophistication and a classic cruise experience embody the spirit of Holland America Line. Perfectly chilled martini glasses that arrive on a gleaming silver tray reflect our attention to detail.

A   V I E W   F R O M

Each evening is a celebration of fine food, which is served on the finest china and in high style in beautifully appointed restaurants and dining rooms.

I FIRST SET FOOT INTO THE GALLEY OF A CRUISE SHIP when I was twenty-two years old. My new job as a sous chef on a vessel berthed in Hamburg, Germany, was the first step in a life I could never have imagined for myself—even in spite of my youthful dreams of traveling the world and leaving forever the landlocked mountain places I had always called home.

Aboard that ship, the *Vistafjord*, my whole vision of life and food changed. While I lived in an extremely confined crew area of the ship, there was somehow a wide-open freedom and excitement I had never known before. Down below the main decks of the *Vistafjord*, we cooks worked long, hard shifts, but the very idea that we were always on the move, always headed to a different destination was thrilling to me.

And then there was the food. At that time, precious few restaurants could afford the high-end ingredients I was able to work with every day

THE GALLEY

on board that ship. For a young chef, it was a kind of nirvana to be working with thousands of lobsters in a week's time, to make beautiful dishes with quail and pheasant on a daily basis. There are no words to describe how privileged I felt to work on board that lovely ship with the best ingredients in the world.

A year later, at age twenty-three, I was offered the position of executive chef on the *Vistafjord*; I accepted and became the youngest-ever executive chef on a cruise liner. That same year, I wrote my first cookbook. Two years later, I became the corporate executive chef of Cunard Line and was also appointed as executive chef on board the famed *Queen Elizabeth II*.

Working as a chef on ships for most of my career has afforded me unique opportunities that I never could have experienced had I been working in land-based kitchens. Traveling the world, I have received an intense education in the global culinary scene and how it has evolved and integrated over time. This is not to mention the fact that I have worked with and met people of all nationalities who have provided invaluable insights into individual tastes and preferences. Needless to say, I have learned an enormous amount.

Twenty-five years later, I am still addicted to my ocean-going life, as driven as ever, still viewing my culinary profession as a race without a finish line, and extremely proud to present you with what is now my ninth cookbook. This book is particularly important to me because it is the first-ever collection of published recipes from Holland America Line, and I feel deeply honored that I was entrusted with presenting it.

Since Holland America Line's maiden voyage in 1873, the company has been an innovative leader of timeless sophistication in the cruise industry. But more than that, it is a company with impeccable integrity, exacting standards, and a deep respect for each and every person on board and for the ocean environment itself. While many well-established organizations rest happily on their laurels, Holland America Line is one of those exceptional forward-thinking companies that extends itself to reach beyond its own borders and dares to imagine that it can exceed even its own greatest achievements. That dynamic quality is the great

Elegant table settings create a perfect stage for memorable meals aboard our ships.

challenge and thrill of working with Holland America Line and what provides unmatched value for its guests.

Being a cook on board any vessel is quite unlike working at a restaurant on land. On a ship, the area where food is cooked is not even called a kitchen, it's known as a galley—an antiquated term, but still one we seafaring cooks will always honor. Furthermore, the cooks sleep, as we say in the trade, "on-premise." For the duration of the cruise, the ship is both home and workplace, which makes the culinary team an extraordinarily close-knit group—which works out exceedingly well because the logistics and fine details of serving well-articulated meals require cohesive teamwork.

At Holland America Line, being a member of the culinary team is especially rewarding because as a company with such a long history, our foundation is in classical cooking technique; however, we have a profound respect for inventiveness. We continually encourage members of our culinary team to experiment, expand their training and horizons, and create an effective interchange of old and new culinary ideas to bring our guests unforgettable dishes that they could experience nowhere else but aboard our ships.

Most of our guests suspect that there must be an army of chefs behind the bounty of extraordinary cuisine we offer during a cruise. These guests might spy the tall white chef hats (toques) that dignify the profession or the flash of white jackets over checked pants might catch the eye of a hungry guest coming into the Lido Restaurant while a buffet is being set.

In fact, there *is* a veritable army chopping, stewing, and firing up the sauté pans; on a ship the military term "brigade" is used to describe the working culinary team. On most of Holland America Line's vessels, the kitchen brigade is made up of one hundred cooks (or, as we like to say, "two hundred hands") plus helpers and dishwashers, each of whom works an average of ten hours a day to coordinate the eleven thousand meals we serve daily. Every Holland America Line ship has its own expert butchers, fishmongers, pastry team, baking team, vegetarian chefs, and so on—all of whom are directed by a single executive chef while the ship is at sea.

But at Holland America Line, we want to do far more than merely serve our guests great food. We want to engage them and immerse them in culinary culture as deeply as they wish to go. We provide our guests with many unique opportunities to learn from our talented chefs, as well work together with guest chefs from *Food & Wine* magazine and other

Culinary inspiration changes by the day as chefs create menus that reflect exotic regional flavors and recipes.

experts that we bring aboard to give lectures, demonstrations, and cooking classes in our Culinary Arts Center. Holland America Line guests leave our cruises not only with a memory of great meals, but armed with the knowledge of how to re-create them at home.

I'd have to say that one of the things I love best about working as the consulting master chef on Holland America Line is that during any given cruise food is not just food, a meal is not just a meal—it's an adventure, it's an event. It is in this spirit that I invite you inside our galley for a seagull's-eye view of a cook's life during the duration of a cruise, as well as the first public glimpses into the distinguished collection of Holland America Line's proprietary signature recipe collection.

May your life, your travels, and your cooking always fill you with the sense of adventure long associated with the rich and excellent traditions of sea travel with Holland America Line.

Happy Cooking! RUDI SODAMIN

Master Chef Rudi Sodamin teaches a cooking class in the new Culinary Arts Center, where guests learn cooking techniques and tricks. They can also become immersed in the world of fine wine.

CHAPTER 1

MORNING MEALS

Whether on land or at sea, the definition of morning is always a personal one. | For some, morning starts predawn, with a deep inhalation and exhalation of breath, and perhaps a stroll to see the sunrise, followed by a healthy meal to begin a new day. | For others, morning on a non-workday is at whatever hour they happen to wake up, and what follows is determined strictly by their mood—breakfast can be anything from a piece of fresh fruit to a full smorgasbord of meats, egg dishes, and rich-grained Danish, cakes, and pancakes. | Then, there are those who, on vacation, will stay in bed dreaming until nearly lunchtime, after the early risers have already put in six hours of activity. Usually these are people who prefer some hot coffee delivered to their rooms, and maybe a little nibble of something while pondering what to have for lunch.

On board our ships, we cater to every personality type and each kind of breakfast ritual. Mornings, the start of a new day with adventures ahead, call for freshness and flexibility, elegance, and abundance. The executive chefs plan their strategies for making this meal special and for satisfying all the tastes and moods of morning.

Breakfast happens for hours aboard each ship, the point of our philosophy being that you can eat what you want, where you want, when you want, and it's all still considered breakfast.

The recipes in this chapter provide something for every taste and every type of morning ritual. Our signature Dutch Apple Pancakes, flavored

A whimsical breakfast menu from 1951 (left) and wine menu from 1960 (right). A glass of wine in 1960 cost thirty cents.

Breakfast

Fruit
Honeydew Melon, Pineapple, Grapefruit, Oranges, Pears, Apples, Bananas
Stewed Prunes and Apricots, Baked Apples, Figs in Syrup
Sliced: Pears-, Pineapple- and Peaches in Cream - Fresh Fruit Salad
Juices: Grapefruit, Prune, Tomato, Pineapple, Orange, Apple, Grape

Cereals
Semouline - Oatmeal - Milkrice
Puffed Rice - Shredded Wheat - Grapenuts - Corn Flakes
All Bran - Puffed Wheat - Rice Krispies

Hot Cakes (7 minutes)
Flapjack-, Buckwheat-, Corn- and Pancakes with Maple Syrup

Fish
Fried Fresh Fish with Lemon - Yarmouth Bloaters - Smoked Haddock

Eggs and Omelets
Boiled-, Fried-, Turned over-, Shirred-, Poached- and Scrambled Eggs
Omelet with: Ham, Bacon, Parsley, Tomato, Mushroom
Jam, Cheese, Veal Kidneys — Omelet Fermière

Meats
Broiled Ham - Fried Bacon

From THE GRILL (15 minutes)
Frankfurter Sausages

Potatoes
Lyonnaise - Boiled

Cold Cuts
Boiled Holland Ham, Lunch Tongue, Minced Veal
Salami-, Tongue-, Cervelate-, Plock-, Parisian- and Farmer Sausages

Relishes
Marinated- and Holland Herring, French Sardines and Tuna Fish in Oil
Mackerel in Oil, Filet of Anchovies

Cheese
Edam - Gouda - Leiden - Gruyère

Preserves
Reine Claude-, Raspberry-, Strawberry-, Cranberry- and Cherry Jam
Guava Jelly, Currant Jelly, Orange Marmalade, Honey, Peanut Butter

Toast
Plain, Milk, Buttered, French, Cinnamon, Dry

Bread
White-, Rye- and Graham Bread
Currant Buns, French- and Sweet Rolls, Graham Rolls, Crescents, Brioches
Raisin- and Corn Muffins, Hot Biscuits, Dutch Rusks, Honey Cake

Beverages
COFFEE: American, HAG, Sanka - Instant Postum, Chocolate, Ovaltine
Fresh Milk, Malted Milk, Buttermilk, Fresh Cream, Yogurt
TEAS: Orange Pekoe, Ceylon, China, Elder Blossom, Camomile

MONDAY, March 19th 1951   R.M.S. "Nieuw Amsterdam"

HOLLAND-AMERICA LINE

RÉGION DE
champagne

the wine steward's suggestion for to day's

LUNCHEON

with your Fried Scallops
POUILLY, per pichet . . . .

with your Grilled Point Steak
MEDOC, per carafe . . . . $ 0.65

with your Cold Entrées
GEWURZTRAMINER, per pichet . . . . $ 0.40

with your Cheeses
SANDEMAN'S PARTNERS PORT, per glass $0.70

S.S. "ROTTERDAM"   FRIDAY, JANUARY 1st 1960 $ 0.30

Holland-America Line

CHAMPAGNE DREAMS

Sandra Scragg, manager beverage revenue and services

Ah, Champagne. The only alcoholic beverage you can drink for breakfast and people won't bat an eye. A topper of bubbly (not to mention premium vodka and fresh squeezed orange juice) makes this Holland America Line original a delight any time of day.

2 slices fresh orange, plus ½ slice for garnish
1½ ounces vodka
1–2 ounces strawberry purée
2 ounces Champagne, chilled

In a pint glass, hand-press 2 orange slices with a muddler. Fill glass with ice. Add vodka and fruit purée. Cap with shaker can and shake well. Strain into a chilled glass and top with Champagne. Garnish with remaining half-slice of orange.   YIELD: 1 DRINK

with maple and honey, are a favorite "Dutch touch" specialty; you will delight your family and guests with an elegant taste of Europe. The Spanish Potato Omelet with tomato salsa will spice up any morning repast, and frankly, the French Toast with Bananas Foster is good enough to be a dessert, for those who crave the sweetest of sweets upon rising.

If you can begin to think about breakfast the way the Holland America Line culinary breakfast team does, you can easily make breakfast special and memorable. It's not that anything is hard, or even particularly fancy, but taking an extra moment to squeeze fresh juice, as we do on board each morning, or to create a beautiful presentation with your oatmeal will be appreciated by family and friends.

Also, you might want to think about eating breakfast in a different room—perhaps on a porch or deck, or around the coffee table in the living room, which can be rendered into a cozy breakfast nook. You can even treat yourself or someone you love to room service—and it doesn't even have to be Mother's Day.

CHEF'S NOTE FROM THE GALLEY

GUENTHER CUSSIGH
Corporate executive chef

To keep cut-up fruit from turning brown before serving, toss with a little lemon juice. You can even put the juice in a spray bottle and dispense that way. The lemon won't truly affect the flavor of your fruit, but it will keep it all looking beautiful and freshly cut.

Dutch Apple Pancakes with Maple Flavored Honey

YIELD: 8–10 MEDIUM PANCAKES

MAPLE HONEY

½ cup maple syrup

½ cup honey

PANCAKES

1½ cups flour

1 tablespoon sugar, plus extra for garnish

2½ teaspoons baking powder

½ teaspoon salt

1 teaspoon ground cinnamon

2 eggs

1½ cups milk

3 tablespoons unsalted butter, melted, plus extra for cooking

2 medium apples, peeled, halved, and cored; plus 2 more for garnish

Make these deliciously moist pancakes during autumn when apples are crisp and plentiful. They're the next best thing to a slice of apple pie for breakfast!

FOR THE MAPLE HONEY

Combine maple syrup and honey in a small serving pitcher; gently stir until mixed. Reserve.

FOR THE PANCAKES

Sift flour, 1 tablespoon sugar, baking powder, salt, and cinnamon together in a large mixing bowl. Put eggs into a medium mixing bowl and beat until frothy. Add milk to eggs and beat well. Add milk mixture to flour mixture and stir to combine. Stir in 3 tablespoons of the melted butter. Using the large holes on a box grater, grate 2 apples into the batter, and stir just to combine.

Heat a large cast-iron skillet over medium heat and swirl in some butter. When the butter is hot but not yet brown, make 2 to 3 pancakes at a time by ladling ¼ cup of the batter for each pancake. Cook until bubbles form on tops of pancakes and bottoms turn golden, 2 to 3 minutes. Flip pancakes and continue cooking until bottoms are golden and centers are cooked through, about 2 minutes more. Repeat process, adding more butter to the pan as necessary. Serve pancakes drizzled with maple honey.

GARNISH

Peel, core, and slice remaining 2 apples into wedges, and sauté in butter with a little sugar until lightly browned. Serve alongside the pancakes.

> TIP | Loosely stack freshly made waffles, pancakes, or French toast on a baking sheet in an oven at 200°F. Cover the stack with damp paper towels so they stay warm and don't dry out. That way everyone can be served at the same time. — **Steve Kirsch**, director, culinary operation

Dutch Waffles with Stewed Strawberry Sauce

Fluffy waffles like these soak up toppings like a sponge, which makes a juicy strawberry sauce the perfect accompaniment.

FOR THE STRAWBERRY SAUCE

In a medium saucepan, combine sugar and water and cook just until sugar melts. Measure out 1 cup sugar syrup and discard the remainder. Pour reserved syrup back into saucepan and add vanilla bean; bring to a boil. Add strawberries, reduce heat, and simmer for 2 minutes. Remove from heat and allow to cool for at least 10 minutes. Remove vanilla bean and set sauce aside.

FOR THE WAFFLES

In a large bowl, thoroughly combine flour, ¼ cup sugar, baking powder, and salt; set aside. In a medium bowl, whisk egg yolks, milk, and oil or butter.

Make a well in the dry ingredients; add the wet ingredients and beat with a fork or hand mixer until smooth (do not overmix).

In a grease-free mixing bowl, beat egg whites with an electric mixer on low speed until frothy. Increase speed to medium and gradually add remaining 2 tablespoons sugar. When sugar is incorporated, increase speed to medium-high and beat until whites hold stiff but not dry peaks. With a rubber spatula, fold whites into waffle batter until well combined.

Lightly coat a waffle iron with vegetable oil spray and preheat it. Pour in enough waffle batter to cover the surface of the iron with a thin layer. Cover the iron.

Cook waffles until steam is no longer emitted, or until the signal light indicates that they're done. Repeat procedure with remaining batter. Serve waffles with reserved strawberry sauce, and garnish with remaining whole berries.

YIELD: 10–12 WAFFLES, 6 INCHES IN DIAMETER

STRAWBERRY SAUCE

¾ cup sugar

¾ cup water

1 small piece vanilla bean (optional)

1 pint strawberries, hulled and sliced, plus additional whole berries for garnish

WAFFLES

1½ cups flour

¼ cup plus 2 tablespoons sugar

1 tablespoon baking powder

1 teaspoon salt

3 eggs, separated

1½ cups milk

½ cup canola oil or melted unsalted butter

Vegetable oil spray

French Toast with Bananas Foster

FRENCH TOAST

1 pint milk

4 eggs

2 tablespoons sugar

Pinch ground cinnamon (optional)

Pinch freshly grated nutmeg
(optional)

Pinch salt

2 tablespoons unsalted butter

10 slices day-old French bread
or challah

BANANAS

⅔ cup unsalted butter, softened

½ cup packed light brown sugar

3 large ripe bananas, sliced

¼ teaspoon cinnamon

⅛ teaspoon freshly ground nutmeg

3 tablespoons dark rum

2 tablespoons banana liqueur

½ teaspoon vanilla extract

Honey for drizzling

Though this elegant variation is simple enough for any day of the year, it makes Mother's Day breakfast a memorable event for everyone. Kids can slice the fruit and dip the bread, while Dad sets the sauce on fire!

FOR THE FRENCH TOAST

In a large bowl combine milk, eggs, sugar, cinnamon, nutmeg, and salt. Whisk until smooth.

Melt 1 tablespoon butter in a frying pan or griddle over medium heat. When butter is hot, dip a slice of bread into the milk mixture, coating each side evenly, and place it in the pan. Repeat with as many slices as will comfortably fit in the pan.

Cook the French toast slices on each side until evenly browned. Repeat procedure with remaining butter, milk mixture, and bread.

FOR THE BANANAS

In a large skillet, heat butter over low heat. Add brown sugar, bananas, cinnamon, and nutmeg. Swirling the skillet back and forth, cook until butter and sugar become creamy and bananas begin to soften, about 1 minute.

Remove skillet from stove and add rum and banana liqueur. While standing back, carefully return skillet to stove and tilt it slightly away from the body to ignite the alcohol. (If you do not have a gas stove, hold a match at the edge of the skillet and tilt it slightly away from the body.) Move skillet back and forth constantly until flames die out. Stir in vanilla and remove from the heat.

Serve French toast with glazed bananas spooned alongside. Drizzle toast with honey and serve.

NOTE

For children, hold the glazed bananas and serve with their favorite French toast topping. Or set aside some sautéed bananas for them before adding the alcohol and igniting.

Spanish Potato Omelet

njoy this hearty omelet hot with toast and bacon for breakfast, warm with a salad for lunch, or cold, cut into small squares, as a late-day nibble with drinks.

In a 10-inch ovenproof skillet, heat 1 tablespoon oil over medium heat until hot but not smoking. Add potatoes and sauté for 10 minutes. Add garlic, peppers, and onion. Sauté until onions turn golden but peppers are still a bit crisp, about 10 minutes. Add the 2 teaspoons mixed herbs and season with salt and pepper to taste. Let cool 5 minutes.

Preheat the broiler. In a medium-size bowl, lightly beat the eggs. Gently stir in cooked vegetables. Heat the remaining 1 tablespoon oil in the skillet over high heat for 1 minute. Add egg mixture and reduce heat to medium so that the omelet starts to cook from the bottom up. After about 4 minutes the surface should be lightly bubbling, indicating that the omelet is cooked three-quarters through.

Sprinkle omelet with cheese. Transfer skillet to broiler and place 6 inches from the flame. Allow omelet to cook until the top starts to brown but not burn. Remove from broiler and let cool for 2 minutes. Ease it out of the skillet onto a plate. Cut into wedges or small squares. Sprinkle with remaining herbs and serve with mustard, if desired.

NOTE

Sliced mushrooms, crumbled Italian sausage, or grated cheese will also make a good addition with the potatoes and onions in this omelet. Tomato salsa (see Pantry Staples) makes a terrific accompaniment.

TIP

Want to know how to tell if an egg is fresh or not? Place the egg in question in a bowl filled with cool salted water. If it's fresh it will sink; if it rises, toss it! —**Robert Hendrix**, executive chef

---

YIELD: 6 SERVINGS

2 tablespoons olive oil

1 pound russet potatoes, peeled and cut into ½-inch cubes

2 large cloves garlic, minced

1 red bell pepper, cored, seeded, and diced

1 green bell pepper, cored, seeded, and diced

½ large onion, peeled and diced

2 teaspoons chopped mixed fresh herbs (oregano, basil, parsley), plus extra for garnish

Salt

Freshly ground black pepper

6 eggs

1 tablespoon grated Parmesan cheese

Mustard (optional)

Sunrise Fitness "Cocktail"

YIELD: 1 SERVING

GRANOLA

2 cups rolled oats

⅓ cup lightly packed light brown sugar

⅓ cup wheat germ

½ cup unsweetened grated coconut

⅓ cup sunflower seeds or cashews

2 tablespoons vegetable oil, plus extra for baking

¼ cup honey

¾ teaspoon vanilla extract

PARFAIT

½ cup fresh berries and diced mixed fresh fruit (such as banana, cantaloupe, or pineapple)

6 ounces (¾ cup) berry yogurt

1 heaping tablespoon granola (see above)

1 tablespoon chopped walnuts, toasted

Mint sprig, for garnish

An elegant wine glass lends a touch of luxury to this refreshing parfait of fresh fruit, yogurt, and granola. Set your table with fancy linen, light a candle or two, and you'll never think of "healthy breakfast" the same way again.

FOR THE GRANOLA

Preheat oven to 325°F. Lightly coat a large baking sheet with oil. In a large bowl, whisk together oats, brown sugar, wheat germ, coconut, and seeds (or cashews). In a small saucepan, heat oil, honey, and vanilla over medium heat until bubbling. Drizzle oat mixture with honey mixture and stir to coat. Spread granola evenly in prepared baking sheet and bake for 15 to 20 minutes, or until lightly golden, stirring once halfway through. Remove from oven, transfer to bowl, and let cool. (Store granola, covered, for up to 1 week in the refrigerator.)

FOR THE PARFAIT

Set aside 1 or 2 pieces of attractive fruit for garnish. In a wine glass, layer half the fruit, half the yogurt, the remaining fruit, and the remaining yogurt. Sprinkle granola and walnuts over the top. Garnish with a mint sprig and reserved fruit. Serve immediately.

NOTE

Feel free to use your favorite store-bought granola in place of homemade.

TIP

Try to incorporate a variety of colorful fruits or vegetables into your breakfast. They not only look appetizing, but they also provide the wide range of the vitamins and minerals your body needs to maintain good health and energy levels. — Tino Daab, executive chef

BREADS & QUICK BREADS

There is nothing like freshly baked bread to bring about a feeling of comfort and to simultaneously deliver the kind of unmatched luxury inherent when presented with anything hand-crafted by an accomplished artist. | Bakers are devoted to a distinctive branch of the culinary profession that demands as much knowledge of science as it does creative artistry. It takes a unique mind with a myriad of skills and a devoted heart to become a true master baker. | Bakers keep some of the oddest hours of any profession, so their particular art form can be appreciated at the height of its flavor and freshness, and the breadmaking artisans on board each Holland America Line ship are no exception. Each ship has four or five master bakers, whose exclusive province (or profession) is to bake all the bread served during a cruise. Rotating shifts, the Holland America Line baking team works around the clock: One team of bakers kneads through the night, so breakfast croissants are flaky and warm. Morning bakers come in to craft the breads for lunch; the afternoon baking team makes dinner rolls fresh every evening at 4 P.M.

On top of it all, these dedicated bakers are also making all of the hamburger and hot dog rolls, biscuits, muffins, specialty breads, and more. To give you some idea of scope, the Holland America Line morning bakers make approximately 100 French baguettes—each formed by hand—every day. The baker's artistry comes both from mind and hand.

Festive menu covers from the thirties feature guests around a table (1936) and couples in the partying spirit (1938).

ULTIMATE BLOODY MARY

Bergado Warlito, bartender

If you think about it, drinking a Bloody Mary—whether for brunch or with your feet up while watching the game— is another way to get a serving of vegetables into your diet.

1 wedge lemon, plus 1 extra wedge for garnish

1½ ounces vodka

½ ounce Bloody Mary mix

2 dashes hot pepper sauce

2 dashes Worcestershire sauce

6 ounces tomato juice

1 olive, for garnish

1 stalk celery, for garnish

1 wedge lime, for garnish

In a pint glass, hand-press 1 lemon wedge with a muddler. Fill glass with ice. Add vodka, Bloody Mary mix, hot pepper sauce, Worcestershire sauce, and tomato juice. Cap with shaker can and shake vigorously. Pour into a pint glass and garnish with olive, celery stalk, lime wedge, and remaining lemon wedge.   YIELD: 1 DRINK

In my cooking classes and demonstrations, I always encourage students to try their hands at making bread. While it assuredly takes a certain mastery to hand-form thousands of rolls a day, it truly takes no special talent to whip up a magnificent blueberry muffin or a fabulous focaccia; and it will not only be appreciated warm out of the oven by your family and guests, but will fill your home with comforting aromas that will become indelible, treasured memories.

The bread recipes you will find in this chapter represent a sampling of the diversity offered from our onboard bakeries. There's a quick-bread muffin for any day; seasoned breads for savory lunches or to add elegance to your dinner party breadbasket; and, of course, the secret recipe for our "Dutch touch" gold standard, Holland America Line's signature Dutch Raisin Rolls, a wonderful yeasty bread roll served around the clock on our ships.

CHEF'S NOTE FROM THE GALLEY

JOHN MULVANEY
Corporate culinary trainer

Save leftover bread products, including bagels, baguettes, biscuits, crackers, rolls, or sandwich bread. Using your food processor or blender, grind up the leftovers into very fine fresh breadcrumbs. Store your breadcrumbs in sealed plastic bags. If you won't need any for a while, they will freeze beautifully. Fresh breadcrumbs, particularly made from a variety of breads, always have better texture and make for a better ingredient than those purchased from a store.

Blueberry Muffins

YIELD: 18 MUFFINS

STREUSEL TOPPING

4 tablespoons unsalted butter

¼ cup sugar

⅔ cup flour

¼ teaspoon vanilla extract

MUFFINS

2¼ cups flour

2 teaspoons baking soda

1½ teaspoons baking powder

1 stick unsalted butter, softened

¾ cup sugar

⅓ cup honey

2 eggs, room temperature

½ teaspoon vanilla extract

1 cup buttermilk, room temperature

2 cups fresh or frozen blueberries
(do not defrost)

For the best results, use the smaller "lowbush" variety of blueberry (often called "wild"), even if frozen is all that's available. Larger "highbush" blueberries are more plentiful and have a longer growing season, but lowbush have a more distinctive flavor and are less likely to sink to the bottom of the muffin.

Preheat oven to 375°F. Lightly oil 18 standard-size muffin cups, place liners in the cups, or coat them with nonstick spray.

FOR THE STREUSEL TOPPING

In a small bowl, combine all ingredients with a fork until mixture is crumbly and looks like coarse meal; set aside.

FOR THE MUFFINS

In a medium bowl, combine flour, baking soda, and baking powder; set aside. In a large bowl, beat butter and sugar until fluffy. Beat in honey, eggs, and vanilla until smooth. Whisk in buttermilk. Add dry ingredients very slowly to wet ingredients, stirring with a rubber spatula until just combined. Fold in blueberries. Spoon batter into prepared muffin cups.

Bake for 15 to 20 minutes, or until the tops are golden and spring back when touched lightly. Let cool in pan for 5 minutes on a wire rack. Loosen the edges and turn muffins out onto rack. Serve warm or at room temperature.

> **TIP** Unlike yeast bread batters, quick bread and muffin batters should be mixed with only a few strokes, just until combined and no more than that. — **Ronald Waasdorp**, executive chef

Dutch Raisin Rolls

T his cheery breadbasket staple enlivens the table from breakfast through dinner, whether served with morning coffee or alongside a savory main course.

In a medium bowl, combine ¾ cup flour, sugar, salt, yeast, and milk. Stir until thoroughly combined. Cover bowl with kitchen towel and set aside in a warm place to let dough rise for 1 hour.

In a small bowl, combine raisins and ⅓ cup hot water. Cover with plastic wrap and allow to sit until softened, stirring once, for 30 minutes. (Don't soak longer or raisins will lose their texture.) Drain raisins, reserving the liquid in a 1-cup liquid measure. Add enough additional liquid to raisin liquid to equal ⅓ cup; reserve.

In the bowl of an electric mixer, place the remaining 3 cups flour, eggs, and 10 tablespoons butter. Add reserved yeast mixture and reserved ⅓ cup raisin liquid. Using the dough hook on the mixer, knead for 10 minutes on low speed, stopping once or twice to scrape down dough as necessary, until dough becomes elastic. Add drained raisins and mix until they are well incorporated into the dough. Cover bowl with kitchen towel and set aside in a warm place to let dough rise for 1 hour.

Preheat oven to 375°F. Lightly grease with butter 2 large baking sheets; set aside. Punch down dough. Turn dough out onto a work surface lightly dusted with flour. Pinch off ¼-cup portions of dough and roll them into balls. Transfer them to prepared baking sheets and cover with kitchen towels. Let rise in a warm place until doubled in bulk, 30 to 40 minutes. Bake for 20 minutes, or until rolls are golden brown and sound hollow when tapped. Brush with soft butter and serve warm.

YIELD: 8 SERVINGS

- 3¾ cups flour, divided
- 3 tablespoons sugar
- ½ tablespoon salt
- 3 (7-gram) packets active dry yeast (6¾ teaspoons)
- 3 ounces whole milk, lukewarm
- ¾ cup raisins
- 2 eggs
- 10 tablespoons unsalted butter, softened, plus extra for greasing and serving

TIP Dough smells faintly of alcohol just after it has risen the first time. Yeast is a single-cell organism that reproduces when it eats the sugars around it. When it divides, it gives off ethyl alcohol and carbon dioxide, a gas that gets trapped in the dough, expanding it. If the dough smells strongly of alcohol, it has risen for too long or at too warm a temperature—make sure its second rise is shorter and/or cooler. — **Rudi Sodamin**, master chef

Garlic Herb Focaccia

SPONGE

¼ cup warm water, 105°–115°F

1 teaspoon active dry yeast

¾ cup sifted flour

GARLIC OIL (SEE NOTE)

6 large cloves garlic, peeled and halved lengthwise

½ cup olive oil

DOUGH

1 teaspoon active dry yeast

1 cup warm water, 105°–115°F

3½ cups sifted flour

2 teaspoons sea salt, plus 1 teaspoon extra for sprinkling

Olive oil, for greasing bowl

1 tablespoon chopped fresh rosemary or thyme leaves

NOTE

Use plain extra virgin olive oil if you don't have time to make homemade garlic oil, or substitute purchased garlic oil. Any leftover garlic oil can be swirled into mashed potatoes or hummus or used in salad dressing.

The name of this popular Italian bread comes from the Latin word *focus*, meaning "hearth," because it was originally baked on a hot stone or under a mound of hot ashes. Follow your fancy with other toppings: caramelized onion, poppy seeds, olives, sun-dried tomatoes, cracked black pepper, even thinly sliced potato.

FOR THE SPONGE

Place water in a small bowl. Stir in yeast. Let stand until yeast dissolves and mixture is cloudy, about 10 minutes. Transfer to the bowl of an electric mixer and stir in flour. Cover with plastic wrap and let stand in a warm place until very bubbly, about 45 minutes.

FOR THE GARLIC OIL

Preheat oven to 300°F. In a small metal bowl or mini loaf pan, combine garlic and olive oil. Bake for 45 minutes. Let cool on a rack for 30 minutes. Strain oil through sieve into a small container. Discard garlic cloves and reserve garlic oil. (Garlic oil may be kept, covered, in the refrigerator for up to 10 days. Do not store at room temperature.)

FOR THE DOUGH

In a small bowl, lightly whisk yeast into warm water. Let stand until yeast dissolves and mixture is cloudy, about 10 minutes. Add dissolved yeast and 3 tablespoons garlic oil to sponge in mixer bowl; with the paddle attachment, mix until well blended. Put the splash guard on the bowl and slowly add flour and 2 teaspoons salt. Mix until thoroughly combined, 1 to 2 minutes. Change to dough hook and knead at medium speed until dough is soft, velvety, and slightly sticky, 3 to 4 minutes. At this point you should be able to pull the dough up into peaks with your fingers. Turn out dough onto lightly floured surface. Knead dough briefly until it comes together. Oil large bowl. Add dough, turning to coat with oil. Cover with plastic wrap. Let dough rise in warm place until doubled, about 1 hour 15 minutes.

Oil base of 10-inch or 12-inch springform pan. Punch down dough. Transfer to prepared springform. Using oiled hands, press out dough to cover bottom of pan. The dough will be sticky and may not cover the bottom of the pan; cover it with a kitchen towel and let it relax for 10 minutes, then stretch it again until it reaches the edges. Cover with kitchen towel. Let rise in warm draft-free area until the dough is full of bubbles, about 1 hour.

Meanwhile, position rack in center of oven. Place baking stone (if you have one) on rack and preheat oven to 425°F. Fill a spritzer bottle

Dill Seed Bread

YIELD: 1 ROUND LOAF

Serve slices of this excellent loaf with any kind of fish chowder. It's also a wonderful treat for the bread basket during the fall and winter holidays.

Dissolve yeast and a pinch of the sugar in water; set aside until foamy. Meanwhile, grease an 8-inch casserole (1½- or 2-quart) with oil; set aside.

In a mixing bowl, combine cottage cheese, the remaining sugar, onion, butter, dill seed, salt, baking soda, egg, and yeast mixture. With a wooden spoon, beat until incorporated. Add 2 cups flour to form a stiff dough, beating well. Turn dough out onto a work surface dusted with ¼ cup flour and knead until almost smooth, 15 to 20 minutes. Transfer dough to a greased bowl; turn to coat. Cover bowl with plastic wrap and set aside in a warm place to let dough rise until light and doubled in size, 50 to 60 minutes.

Preheat oven to 350°F. Punch down dough. Transfer to prepared casserole. Let rise in a warm place until doubled in bulk, 30 to 40 minutes. Bake for 40 to 50 minutes, or until golden brown and bread sounds hollow when tapped. Brush with soft butter and sprinkle with salt.

1 (7-gram) packet active dry yeast (2¼ teaspoons)

2 tablespoons sugar

¼ cup warm water, 105°–115°F

1 cup cottage cheese, creamed and heated to lukewarm

1 tablespoon dried minced onion

1 tablespoon unsalted butter, softened, plus extra for greasing and brushing

2 teaspoons dill seed

1 teaspoon salt, plus extra for sprinkling

¼ teaspoon baking soda

1 egg

2¼ cups flour, plus ¼ cup extra if needed

> TIP   To be certain your bread is done, insert an instant-read thermometer in the bottom center of the loaf—if it reads over 200°F, it's done. — **Guenther Cussigh**, corporate executive chef

with cold water. Using fingertips, press dough all over, creating dimples. Drizzle dough with 2 tablespoons garlic oil and sprinkle with rosemary (or thyme) and remaining 1 teaspoon salt. Place pan directly on pizza stone. Spray oven walls and floor with cold water. Bake until crust is crisp and top is golden, about 20 to 25 minutes. (You may remove focaccia from pan and bake it directly on the baking stone for the last 10 minutes.) Remove focaccia from pan immediately and let cool on wire rack. Serve warm or at room temperature.

CHAPTER 3

APPETIZERS

On all Holland America Line menus, the offerings for appetizers are artistic and eclectic. As a culinary team we not only must satisfy the most basic cravings of guests seeking simple, elegant, and subtle preludes to meals. We also must meet the highest expectations of guests interested in gustatory experiences that inspire the imagination as well as the appetite. | The little tastes, different flavors, and opportunities for creative presentation afforded by the appetizer course is designed to signal to all who are dining that what will follow will be a leisurely event designed to delight. Personally and professionally speaking, these appetizers are intended not only to beautifully fill the time while the main courses are being prepared, but to spark conviviality and conversation. In fact, many of my appetizer recipes for Holland America Line have the word dialogue in the title of the dish, like the Dialogue of Smoked Salmon Tartare with Guacamole and Tomato Salsa.

Incorporating appetizers into your repertoire for weeknight cooking as well as for entertaining is a terrific idea. It's a healthful habit, as we are all likely to eat a little less of a rich main course if we've had a satisfying starter, plus appetizers give opportunities for introducing new cuisines, ingredients, and taste experiences in a more accessible way.

We selected primarily seafood appetizer recipes for this chapter to reflect your time at sea with Holland America Line. Elsewhere in the book, you'll find chapters devoted to salads, soups, and sandwiches and snacks, all of which can be translated into excellent appetizer options.

Menus from 1911 have a Delft-tile theme. The cover for a lunch menu is from the *Rotterdam* (bottom); the *Ryndam* dinner menu is from Monday, November 6.

GREEN APPLE MARTINI

Caqderes Kristoferson, bartender

Neon green and vividly tangy and sweet, this drink is made to share with friends.

2 lemon wedges

1 ounce vodka

1 ounce green apple schnapps

1½ ounces homemade sour mix (see Pantry Staples)

1 slice apple, for garnish

In a pint glass, hand-press lemon wedges with a muddler. Fill glass with ice. Add liquors and sour mix. Cap with shaker can and shake vigorously. Strain into a chilled martini glass. Garnish with apple slice. YIELD: 1 DRINK

The basic techniques of the seafood recipes in this chapter are all the same, making them as versatile as they are delicious and dynamic. If you don't have crab meat for the Dungeness Crab Cakes with Lime Ginger Sauce, for example, simply substitute salmon meat, or if you are in the mood for lobster, and can get your hands on some spectacular lobster meat, by all means, make lobster cakes. No matter which ingredients you use, create a presentation for your appetizer designed to dazzle; feel free to take your inspiration from the photographs of how we present these dishes on board.

Our guests will often ask how the Holland America Line culinary team can consistently turn out such stunning and tasty appetizers in the volume required to serve seatings of hundreds of guests. Indeed, it takes major orchestration of talent and logistics behind the galley doors. The secret on our ships is to have one cook dedicated to making a single appetizer selection on the menu; he or she makes it beautifully, arranges it the same way on the plate each time, and the expression of the recipe and the presentation of the dish is completely and consistently individual— just the way it will be for you at home.

CHEF'S NOTE FROM THE GALLEY

GUIDO SCARPELLINO
Corporate culinary trainer

If you don't have a deep-fat thermometer, in a pinch try this trick for gauging temperature: For deep-fat frying, drop a cube of white bread into the hot oil. If it browns evenly in 60 seconds, then the temperature of the oil is 350 to 365°F, in 40 seconds, 365 to 382°F, in 20 seconds, 382 to 390°F.

Dialogue of Smoked Salmon Tartare with Guacamole and Tomato Salsa

YIELD: 8 SERVINGS

PICKLED SALMON

8 ounces skinless salmon fillet

¼ teaspoon minced garlic

¼ teaspoon minced fresh rosemary

¼ teaspoon minced fresh dill

½ jalapeño pepper, minced

1½ cups white distilled vinegar

½ teaspoon olive oil

½ teaspoon pickling spices

½ cup sugar

1 cup water

½ medium onion, cut into ¼-inch slices

CHIPOTLE HOT-SMOKED SALMON

4 ounces skinless salmon fillet

¼ teaspoon kosher salt

¼ teaspoon sugar

¼ teaspoon sweet paprika (not hot)

⅛ teaspoon chipotle chile powder

TO ASSEMBLE

8 ounces cold-smoked salmon slices

1 avocado, split, with ½ cut into small uniform dice and ½ reserved for garnish

1½ teaspoons fresh lemon juice, plus 8 slices lemon for garnish

1 tomato, seeded and cut into small uniform dice

½ teaspoon finely chopped cilantro, plus 8 extra sprigs cilantro for garnish

1½ teaspoons extra virgin olive oil, plus extra for oiling molds and drizzling plate

1½ teaspoons balsamic vinegar

8 tablespoons sour cream, for garnish

Sure to hook the salmon shy, and rekindle the romance of the millions of salmon lovers out there, this popular Holland America Line signature dish celebrates our favorite fish three ways: cold-smoked, pickled, and chipotle hot-smoked. Plan accordingly, as this "salmon spectacular" requires day-ahead preparation.

FOR THE PICKLED SALMON

Cut salmon into 1½-inch cubes. Place in nonreactive bowl with garlic, herbs, and jalapeño; set aside. Meanwhile, in a 2-quart nonreactive saucepan, combine remaining ingredients and bring to a boil over medium heat. Immediately pour vinegar mixture over salmon in bowl. Cover and refrigerate for 24 hours.

FOR THE CHIPOTLE HOT-SMOKED SALMON

Place salmon in a flat glass dish. Combine remaining ingredients and rub both sides of the salmon evenly with it. Chill, covered, for 2 hours. Build a smoky fire by adding soaked hickory chips to medium-hot coals. Place salmon on grill and close the top. Cook for 5 minutes and then flip fillet and cook for 5 minutes more with the top closed. (Alternatively, hot-smoke salmon in a stovetop smoker over alder wood chips on a medium-low burner; cook for 5 minutes then turn off the burner and let smoker cool, closed, for 5 minutes.) Remove salmon and chill, covered, until cold.

TO ASSEMBLE

Take half the cold-smoked salmon slices and cut them so you have 8 small slices. Transfer to a plate, cover, and chill until needed. Finely dice remaining cold-smoked salmon slices and place in a nonreactive bowl. Drain reserved pickled salmon, removing onion and any large spices, and add to the bowl. Dice reserved hot-smoked chipotle salmon and add to the bowl. Gently toss all 3 salmons together, cover, and chill until needed. Gather 3 small bowls. In the first, gently toss diced avocado with 1 teaspoon lemon juice; set aside. In the second, mash remaining avocado half and remaining ½ teaspoon lemon juice until smooth; set aside. In the third, gently toss tomato, chopped cilantro, 1½ teaspoons olive oil, and balsamic vinegar; set aside.

TO SERVE

Rub olive oil generously inside a 1½-inch metal ring or small can (such as a tomato paste can with the top and bottom removed) and place ring on plate. Spoon some salmon mixture into ring and press down gently with your finger or a spoon while lifting the ring slightly away from the plate,

to unmold salmon. Repeat with remaining mixture. For each serving: curl a small slice of reserved smoked salmon on top of tower; spoon some reserved diced avocado and diced tomato salsa alongside; garnish with 1 spoonful each of mashed avocado and sour cream; drizzle plate with some extra virgin olive oil and serve immediately.

NOTE

If you have difficulty unmolding the salmon tower, line the oiled ring or can with a strip of parchment paper before filling; remove parchment from salmon tower after unmolding.

Carpaccio of Seared Ahi Tuna with Papaya-Ginger Relish and Fried Ginger Chips

The sweet and savory relish accompanying the tuna is also delicious served with grilled chicken or pork.

FOR THE PAPAYA-GINGER RELISH

In a nonreactive saucepan, combine onion, pepper, ginger, brown sugar, allspice, cloves, salt, vinegar, and corn syrup over medium-high heat. Cook at a rapid boil, stirring occasionally, until mixture is an amber color and syrupy, about 12 minutes. Add currants and papaya and continue to boil, stirring gently to keep fruit pieces intact, until thick, about 4 minutes. Immediately pour relish out into a wide shallow pan to cool down quickly. Remove and discard whole cloves. When cool, transfer relish to a nonreactive bowl, cover, and chill until needed.

FOR THE CARPACCIO

Divide tuna slices among 4 large plates, neatly arranging them in a single layer. Wrap tightly with plastic and refrigerate until needed. In a small bowl, whisk peppercorns, juices, soy sauce, and olive oil. Cover and chill until needed.

TO SERVE

For each serving, unwrap a plate of tuna and brush the surface gently with reserved peppercorn mixture. Spoon a mound of reserved papaya relish in center of plates. Garnish with fried ginger, if desired, and serve immediately.

NOTE

To crisply fry thin slices of peeled ginger, heat 4 tablespoons vegetable oil in a small cast-iron skillet until hot but not smoking. Add ginger slices and fry until golden brown and crisp. Remove with a slotted spoon and blot on paper towels.

YIELD: 4 SERVINGS

PAPAYA-GINGER RELISH

1 tablespoon diced red onion

2 tablespoons diced red bell pepper

2 tablespoons minced fresh ginger

4 tablespoons light brown sugar

Dash ground allspice

4 whole cloves

Dash kosher salt

4 tablespoons white wine vinegar

4 tablespoons light corn syrup

2 tablespoons dried currants

2 ripe but firm papayas, peeled and cut into ½-inch dice

CARPACCIO

12 ounces skinless sushi-grade ahi tuna, very thinly sliced

2 tablespoons pink peppercorns, coarsely crushed

Juice of ½ small orange

Juice of 1 small lime

1 tablespoon soy sauce

2 teaspoons olive oil

8 slices crispy fried ginger, for garnish (optional; see Note)

Mariners' Seafood Cocktail

YIELD: 2–10 SERVINGS

POACHING LIQUID

1 gallon water

¼ cup fresh lemon juice

2 tablespoons salt

2 teaspoons black peppercorns

2 bay leaves

SEAFOOD

Large shrimp, peeled and deveined (1–2 per serving)

Bay scallops (5 per serving)

Squid, cleaned and sliced in ½-inch pieces (6 ounces per serving)

Crab claws or legs (1 per serving)

Fully cooked lobster meat (2 ounces per serving)

Fully cooked crab meat (2 ounces per serving)

Mussels, steamed in their shells and chilled (2 per serving)

SAUCE AND GARNISH

Cocktail sauce of your choice or guacamole (optional; see Pantry Staples)

Salsa (optional; see Pantry Staples)

Lemon wedges, for garnish

This showstopper requires the freshest seafood you can find. Choose any variety you enjoy and match your catch with a zingy, lip-smacking sauce.

In a large saucepan, combine poaching liquid ingredients and bring to a boil. Add shrimp (if using) and simmer just until done. Remove shrimp with a strainer, place in a bowl, cover, and refrigerate for at least 1 hour. Repeat with scallops, squid, and crab claws/legs—whichever you are using. Coarsely chop lobster meat (if using) and chill. Drain crab meat well (if using) and pick out any shell pieces; reserve chilled.

For each serving, spoon some cocktail sauce (or guacamole) into a goblet. Top with cooked seafood of your choice attractively arranged. (If using guacamole, spoon some salsa over the top.) Serve immediately garnished with lemon wedges.

NOTE

For even more flavor, toss cooked seafood with a marinade before arranging in the goblet. For a guacamole cocktail, toss seafood with a mixture of orange juice, lime juice, and finely chopped cilantro.

TIP

Foods with the julienne cut (⅛-inch-wide matchsticks, 2 inches to 4 inches long) are very attractive but easily overcook, which is why they are most often used as garnish. To cut food into a julienne, first cut it into ⅛-inch slices and then stack the slices and again slice in ⅛-inch pieces. —**Joachim Barrelman**, executive chef

Dungeness Crab Cakes with Lime Ginger Sauce

YIELD: 8 SERVINGS

CUCUMBER DRESSING

⅓ cup white wine vinegar

⅓ cup sugar

¾ teaspoon salt

½ tablespoon ground cardamom

½ tablespoon ground allspice

CRAB CAKES

½ cup finely diced celery

½ onion, finely diced

1 medium red bell pepper, finely diced

3 cups cooked Dungeness crab meat, well drained and picked over

2 eggs

1 cup mayonnaise

Juice of ½ lemon

1 teaspoon Worcestershire sauce

⅓ teaspoon hot pepper sauce

1 tablespoon minced chives

1 teaspoon minced fresh thyme

1 teaspoon minced fresh garlic

Salt

Freshly ground black pepper

1½ cups panko or bread crumbs (see Notes)

C ooked lobster meat or halibut make terrific substitutes for crab meat in this recipe. Use any leftover lime ginger sauce on seared salmon fillets.

FOR THE CUCUMBER DRESSING

Combine all ingredients in a large heavy pan. Bring to a boil, stirring to dissolve the sugar. Boil for 1 minute. Remove from the heat and let cool. Cover and refrigerate until needed.

FOR THE CRAB CAKES

In a large bowl, gently fold together all ingredients except salt, pepper, and panko. Add salt and pepper to taste and sauté a small portion to test for seasoning. Generously sprinkle some panko on a baking sheet. Scoop out mounds of crab mixture with an ice cream scoop and place on prepared baking sheet. One by one, dredge mounds in remaining panko, shaping into cakes as you go. Cover and refrigerate until needed.

FOR THE LIME GINGER SAUCE

In a heavy saucepan over medium heat, combine sake, lime juice, vinegar, ginger, and garlic. Bring to a boil; reduce by 90 percent to a light syrup. Add cream and reduce by 60 percent, stirring carefully so as not to scorch the sauce. Reduce heat to low and gradually whip in the cold butter chunks. Whisk in chili sauce. Season with salt and pepper. Reserve and keep warm.

NOTES

- Japanese bread crumbs, called panko, are coarse in texture and often used for frying because they create a deliciously crunchy crust. Panko is sold in Asian markets and often in the seafood section of large supermarkets. If panko is unavailable, plain dry bread crumbs may be substituted.

- Be sure you purchase sweet chili sauce and not the hot sauce variety. Sometimes the label says Thai Sweet Chili Sauce "for Chicken."

- If you do not have a spiral slicer, cut cucumber in half lengthwise and use a Y-shaped vegetable peeler to peel very thin wide ribbons of cucumber along the cut side of each half.

LIME GINGER SAUCE

1 cup sake

¼ cup fresh lime juice

⅓ cup white wine vinegar

1 tablespoon minced fresh ginger

1 tablespoon minced fresh garlic

½ cup heavy cream

1½ sticks cold unsalted butter, cut into chunks

¼ cup Thai sweet chili sauce (see Notes)

Kosher salt

Freshly ground white pepper

TO ASSEMBLE

¼ cup clarified butter

1 tablespoon Thai sweet chili sauce

½ seedless European cucumber, unpeeled and well scrubbed, cut into curly shavings on a spiral slicer (see Notes)

2 tablespoons chives snipped in ¼-inch lengths, plus 16 (5-inch-long) whole chives

TO SERVE

Heat some clarified butter in a nonstick griddle over medium-high heat until hot but not smoking. Add as many crab cakes as will fit in the griddle comfortably. Sauté until golden brown and heated through, about 4 minutes per side. Remove to paper towels and drain. Divide among warm plates.

TO GARNISH

Spoon 3 small pools of reserved lime ginger sauce on each plate. With a toothpick or skewer, drop a dot of Thai sweet chili sauce into the middle of each lime sauce pool. Curl thin cucumber slices in a pile on each crab cake. Sprinkle cucumber with some reserved dressing and snipped chives. Lean long chive strands on each crab cake and serve immediately.

Watermelon "Cocktail" with Orange and Mint Syrup

Wake up your palate—and your appetite!—with this beautiful and refreshing starter. Drizzle any leftover syrup on waffles or pancakes, brush it on chocolate cake layers before frosting, or stir it into iced tea.

Using a vegetable peeler, remove orange part of peel from orange in long strips. Cut peel lengthwise into ⅛-inch-wide strips; set aside.

In a saucepan, combine sugar, water, orange concentrate, corn syrup, and chopped mint. Bring to a boil over medium heat, stirring until sugar is dissolved. Simmer syrup for 3 minutes. Carefully pour syrup through a fine sieve into a bowl or large glass measuring cup, pressing on mint leaf solids. Stir reserved orange peel into hot syrup and let cool to room temperature. (Syrup will keep, covered, in the refrigerator for up to one week.)

Cut watermelon in half and remove seeds, if necessary. Scoop watermelon into balls with a melon baller and place in a bowl. Gently toss watermelon with enough reserved orange syrup to coat. Spoon about 10 watermelon balls into each large martini glass and garnish with mint sprigs.

NOTE

You may use high-quality frozen orange juice concentrate for this recipe, just seek out one that is pulp free. For a quicker orange syrup, toss watermelon balls with a combination of honey, fresh orange juice, and fresh chopped mint.

TIP

Because appetizer portions are smaller, they need garnishes to keep the plate from looking too bare. Fill space with frisée, radicchio, or red leaf lettuce. Add geometric interest with a cross-hatch of chive strands or small dots of sauce. Echo ingredients by arranging herb sprigs, citrus peel cut into matchsticks, or small diced tomato on the plate. Even coarsely crushed black peppercorns and sea salt encircling the food will make a difference. —**Bernie Rius**, executive chef

---

YIELD: 8 SERVINGS

1 orange, washed well

1 cup sugar

1 cup water

½ cup orange concentrate (see Note)

3 tablespoons light corn syrup

2 bunches (1 cup) fresh mint leaves, chopped, plus whole mint sprigs for garnish

1 medium red watermelon

CHAPTER 4

SOUP

If ever there was a match made in heaven between food and setting, it is soup and the sea. Back when sea travel was far less luxurious than it is today, mugs of hot steaming bouillon were passed around to seafarers to keep all hands on deck warm.　　At Holland America Line, we keep this excellent tradition of life at sea very much alive: The signature Dutch Pea Soup has circled the globe for centuries with travelers. Aboard our cruises, this famous soup is a beloved tradition for guests enjoying our Alaskan and European itineraries. The romance of cruising in cooler climates is captured in an instant when our servers proffer steaming mugs of this rich savory soup to warm the hands of our guests.

MOJITO

Nicanor Torrano, bartender

Truly one of the planet's most sublimely refreshing cocktails. Holland America Line's rendition includes a splash of lemon-lime soda.

2 wedges lime

3 sprigs mint, plus 1 extra for garnish

1½ ounces light rum

1½ ounces homemade sour mix (see Pantry Staples)

1½ ounces soda water

1 splash lemon-lime soda

In a pint glass, hand-press lime wedges with a muddler. Tear 3 mint sprigs and drop in. Fill glass with ice. Add rum, sour mix, soda water, and lemon-lime soda. Cap with shaker can and shake vigorously for 8 seconds. Pour into a pint glass and garnish with remaining mint sprig. Serve with a straw.   YIELD: 1 DRINK

ED SAYOMAC
Executive chef

Too much salt? If you are cooking a soup or stew and accidentally over-salt, cut one or two potatoes into large chunks and add them to the pot. The potatoes will absorb a good percentage of the excess salt. Remove the potatoes before serving your soup or stew.

Far below deck, soup is simmering away in gleaming silver soup kettles 24/7. There are cooks who are responsible for making every type of soup offered on all of our menus. If you loved the Dutch Pea Soup, or feel like you will never forget one of Holland America Line's signature chilled soups, the cook who made it during that cruise can truly take credit.

And you can too! One of the easiest meals to make (and among the most satisfying foods to cook and eat), soup is also versatile: it can certainly be a meal in and of itself; it makes a tasty appetizer or first course; or, if making a chilled fruit soup, it can be a memorable and distinctive dessert.

What's great about these soups is that they all can be made ahead of time, so you can focus attention on presenting them with flair as we do.

So, whether hot or cold, classic or *nuevo*, served in a rustic pottery crock or in a fine china teacup, soup is sure to satisfy your urge to nurture, to create, and to celebrate.

Chilled Raspberry Soup

his festive, refreshing chilled soup is a great way to kick off an
alfresco dinner of grilled meats in the summertime.

YIELD: 6 SERVINGS

2 pints fresh raspberries, gently
washed

2 cups sour cream

1 cup whole milk

1 cup ginger ale

¼ cup sugar

2 tablespoons triple sec

2 tablespoons fresh lemon juice

Reserve 6 raspberries for garnish. In a blender or food processor, purée
the remaining raspberries until smooth. Strain the mixture through a fine
sieve over a nonreactive bowl, pushing through as much of the pulp as
you can, leaving the seeds behind.

Whisk the remaining ingredients, except for the reserved berries,
into the purée. Cover and refrigerate until cold. To serve, divide the soup
among chilled bowls and garnish with the reserved raspberries.

VARIATION

For chilled blueberry soup, substitute blueberries for the raspberries and
the same quantity of champagne for the triple sec.

Chilled Sour Cherry Soup with Crème Fraîche and Fried Ginger

FRIED GINGER

1 cup water

1 cup sugar

⅓ cup thin slices of fresh ginger

2 cups canola oil

SOUR CHERRY SOUP

2 pounds fresh or frozen sour cherries, pitted

1 cup water

10 star anise, cracked

½ teaspoon grated orange zest

¾ cup black currant vinegar (available from gourmet food stores)

TO ASSEMBLE

¾ cup crème fraîche, store-bought or homemade (see Pantry Staples)

20 fresh sour cherries, pitted and halved

10 leaves fresh mint, very thinly sliced

1 tablespoon honey

½ teaspoon grated orange zest

Tart and sweet, this heady combination of flavors—like a good aperitif—will prime your palate for a spectacular meal.

FOR THE FRIED GINGER

In a small saucepan, combine water and sugar over medium heat. Cook, stirring, until sugar dissolves. Bring mixture to a simmer. Add ginger and cook, stirring, for 3 minutes. Strain ginger and pat it dry on paper towels.

In a thick-bottomed pan or cast-iron skillet, heat oil to 350°F. (A small piece of bread dropped into the oil should float to the surface almost immediately and brown within 45 seconds.) Deep-fry ginger until golden brown, about 2 minutes. Drain on paper towels and reserve.

FOR THE SOUR CHERRY SOUP

Put cherries through a juicer, reserving both juice and pulp separately. In a small saucepan, combine water, star anise, and orange zest. Place over medium heat and bring to a simmer. Cook, stirring occasionally, for 10 minutes. Strain through a fine sieve into a nonreactive bowl.

Stir in reserved cherry juice. Tasting as you go, slowly add vinegar, stopping when a balanced flavor is reached. Cover and refrigerate until cold.

TO ASSEMBLE

In a medium bowl, whisk crème fraîche until somewhat lightened. With a rubber spatula, fold in 2 to 3 tablespoons of the reserved cherry pulp. Cover and refrigerate until cold.

In another medium bowl, combine halved cherries, mint, honey, and orange zest. Cover and refrigerate until cold.

TO SERVE

Divide cherry crème fraîche, minted cherries, and fried ginger among chilled soup bowls. Gently ladle cherry soup around garnishes and serve immediately.

Apple and Pear Gazpacho
with Ice Wine Sorbet

A merica's favorite pear, the Bartlett, was developed in England by a horticulturist named Williams. When its seedlings crossed over with the early colonists, though, it was "rediscovered" and renamed by a Massachusetts nurseryman named Bartlett, who was unaware of its true origin. Ever since, the pear has been known as the Bartlett in the U.S., but is still referred to as the Williams pear in other parts of the world.

FOR THE ICE WINE SORBET

In a nonreactive saucepan, combine all the ingredients and bring to a boil over medium-high heat. Boil for 3 minutes and then cool. Taste liquid: add water or a little unsweetened apple juice if too sweet. Transfer to a sorbet maker and freeze according to manufacturer's instructions. (If you don't have a sorbet machine, place liquid on a shallow tray and then freeze; once frozen, scrape crystals into a blender and blend until smooth. Transfer resulting slush to a plastic container, cover, and return to freezer.)

FOR THE APPLE AND PEAR GAZPACHO

In a large skillet, heat butter over medium-high heat. Add sliced apples, diced pears, citrus juices, and vanilla bean. Cook a little, allowing apples and pears to meld with butter, then add apple juice and cinnamon. When fruits are tender, remove from heat, cool slightly, and remove vanilla bean. Transfer to a container and stir in crème fraîche and lemon balm. Cover and refrigerate until cold. To serve, spoon into shallow bowls, garnish with slices of remaining apple and pear, and top with a scoop of ice wine sorbet and a lemon balm sprig.

> TIP | For the best flavor, delicate fresh fruit soups should be enjoyed as soon after they're made as possible. Most other soups, however, improve with age and can be made a day or two in advance or can be frozen to enjoy later. —**Ian Thomson**, executive chef

YIELD: 8 SERVINGS

ICE WINE SORBET

2 cups ice wine

1 cup sugar

1 tablespoon fresh lemon juice

APPLE AND PEAR GAZPACHO

1 tablespoon unsalted butter

2 Golden Delicious apples, peeled, cored, and sliced, plus 1 extra for garnish

2 Bartlett (or Williams) pears, peeled, cored, and diced, plus 1 extra for garnish

Juice of 1 lemon

Juice of ½ lime

½ vanilla bean

2 cups unsweetened apple juice

Pinch ground cinnamon

½ cup crème fraîche, store-bought or homemade (see Pantry Staples)

6 lemon balm leaves, shredded, plus extra sprigs for garnish

Black Bean Soup with Mango Relish

YIELD: 6 SERVINGS

MANGO RELISH

1 mango, peeled and finely diced

½ red bell pepper, chopped

½ bunch scallions, white and tender green portions only, thinly sliced

½ bunch flat-leaf parsley, chopped

1 teaspoon finely chopped cilantro

Juice of 1 lime

BLACK BEAN SOUP

4 teaspoons olive oil

4 slices bacon, diced

½ Spanish onion, chopped

3 cloves garlic, minced

1 teaspoon ground cumin

1 cup black beans, soaked overnight

10½ cups vegetable stock, canned or homemade (see Pantry Staples), plus extra for thinning soup

1 tablespoon red wine vinegar

½ teaspoon salt

½ teaspoon freshly ground black pepper

This Cuban-style soup is also delicious served with rice: Unmold a ramekin of cooked rice into a shallow soup bowl, pour the soup around, and top the rice with the mango relish.

FOR THE MANGO RELISH

In a small nonreactive bowl, combine all ingredients. Cover and refrigerate until needed.

FOR THE BLACK BEAN SOUP

In a heavy 4-quart saucepan, heat oil over medium heat. Add bacon, onion, and garlic; sauté until onion is translucent, about 3 minutes. Stir in cumin and cook a few seconds more.

Add dried beans, stock, vinegar, and salt. Bring to a simmer and cook until beans are tender, about 40 minutes. Let cool slightly. With a slotted spoon, remove some black beans and reserve for garnish. Transfer remaining contents of saucepan in batches to a blender. Purée until smooth, adding additional stock if soup is too thick. Reheat and adjust seasoning, adding black pepper. Spoon into soup bowls and garnish with mango relish and reserved whole cooked black beans.

> **TIP** A blender works better than a food processor or a food mill for puréeing soups. Food processors tend to leak around the motor shaft when filled more than halfway with hot soup, and food mills have a hard time breaking down fibrous ingredients. To avoid burns, always remember to let your soup cool down a bit before puréeing it. —**Dennis Starch**, executive chef

Dutch Pea Soup (*Snert*)

Dutch cuisine is famous for Gouda cheese and *maatjesharing* (young herring eaten slightly salted but essentially raw), but the pea soup called *snert* is an icon. It has many variations, but is usually very thick and contains pork. To achieve the correct consistency, make the soup a day in advance and then reheat it.

Rinse split peas in a sieve under running water. In a soup pot, bring 2 quarts water, peas, ham steak (or other pork product), and bacon to a boil. Skim off any floating scum. Remove meat with tongs and strain peas from liquid, discarding liquid. Rinse peas again and return them and meat to empty pot. Add 2 quarts fresh water and bring to a simmer over medium heat.

After peas and meat reach a gentle simmer, add onion, carrot, leek, celeriac, and potato to pot and continue to simmer. After 1½ hours, add whole smoked sausage (or frankfurters) and celery leaves and sprigs. When peas are soft and broken down (about 2 hours total cooking time), take meat out of pot with tongs, remove rind and bones, and cut meat into small pieces. Return meat to pot. Season soup with salt and pepper and remove from the heat.

The pea soup will still be fairly liquid; let it cool completely and reheat it the next day (see Note), removing the whole sausage (or frankfurters) first and slicing it thinly before returning it to the soup.

To serve, ladle soup into large bowls and serve with bread.

NOTE

Reheat smaller portions of soup in a microwave and larger portions in an ovenproof pot in a moderate oven, stirring occasionally, or on top of the stove over low heat, stirring occasionally, so the bottom doesn't burn.

YIELD: 12 SERVINGS

1 pound green split peas
(do not soak)

1 gallon water, plus extra as needed

½ pound pork product (ham steak, pork hock, or spareribs) or
2 pigs' feet

½ pound unsmoked streaky bacon or pork, preferably with rind

1 large onion, diced

1 large carrot, peeled and diced

1 leek, white and light green parts only, well washed and diced

1 celery root, peeled and diced

1 potato, peeled and diced

½ pound smoked pork sausage or frankfurters

Leaves and inner sprigs only from 1 bunch celery, coarsely chopped

Salt

Freshly ground black pepper

White bread or pumpernickel, as an accompaniment

Roasted Shallot and Butternut Squash Soup with Beet Crisps

YIELD: 8 SERVINGS

BEET CRISPS

1 large beet, peeled

1 cup vegetable oil

Flaked sea salt

BUTTERNUT SQUASH SOUP

2 tablespoons unsalted butter

2 cups shallots, peeled and halved

4 cloves garlic, peeled

2 large butternut squash,
peeled and cut into 1-inch dice

4 tablespoons maple syrup,
plus extra if needed

½ teaspoon ground allspice

Pinch freshly grated nutmeg

3 cups vegetable stock, canned or
homemade (see Pantry Staples)

½ cup heavy cream

1 sprig thyme, stem removed

Salt

Freshly ground black pepper

S low cooking brings out the natural sweetness of the shallots in this creamy soup that's rich with fall flavors.

FOR THE BEET CRISPS

With a mandolin (or a potato peeler if you don't have a mandolin), slice beet very thinly. In a thick-bottomed pan or cast-iron skillet, heat oil to 350°F. (A small piece of bread dropped into the oil should float to the surface almost immediately and brown within 45 seconds.) Preheat oven to 180°F. Deep-fry small batches of beet slices until slightly browned at the edges. Remove with a slotted spoon and drain on paper towels. Season with sea salt. Place on a baking sheet in oven to dry out for an hour or so, or leave overnight in a warmed oven that has been turned off.

FOR THE BUTTERNUT SQUASH SOUP

In a thick-bottomed soup pot, heat butter over medium-low heat. Add shallots and garlic. Cook very slowly, stirring gently, until vegetables are golden brown. Add squash, 4 tablespoons maple syrup, allspice, and nutmeg; cook slowly, covered, until squash begins to soften and all the vegetables are coated in syrup.

Add stock and cream and bring to a light simmer. Add thyme and season with salt and pepper. Adjust with more maple syrup, if required. Let cool slightly and purée in batches in blender. Return to the pot and check the seasoning once more.

Serve in bowls and sprinkle with beet crisps just before serving.

CHAPTER 5

SALADS & DRESSINGS

I will always marvel at the culinary miracle of even the simplest salad served at sea. | It is a luxury to be in the middle of the ocean—miles away from fields where salad ingredients grow—and to pierce with a silver fork a piece of frisée as fresh and crisp as you've ever encountered. Keeping produce fresh on a ship is quite an accomplishment, and it happens on every Holland America Line cruise. | The storage conditions of greens, herbs, and spices must be carefully tended to and controlled. The whole storage routine, combined with weekly provisioning, is a logistical wonder. | Then there's the matter of making all the hundreds of individual salads we serve daily. We make all our salads in what is called the cold kitchen. There

COSMO CUBANO

Willy Reyes, bartender

This perfect, clean and refreshing libation is a loyal partner for any occasion, at any time, at any place.

2 wedges lime

3 sprigs mint, plus 1 extra sprig for garnish

1½ ounces pineapple rum

1½ ounces homemade sour mix (see Pantry Staples)

1 ounce cranberry juice

In a pint glass, hand-press lime wedges with a muddler. Tear 3 mint sprigs and drop in. Fill glass with ice. Add rum, sour mix, and cranberry juice. Cap with shaker can and shake vigorously. Strain into a chilled martini glass. Garnish with remaining mint sprig.

YIELD: 1 DRINK

RAYMOND SOUTHERN
Executive chef

Delicate salad greens require light vinaigrettes. Make any vinaigrette lighter by whisking a couple of teaspoons of boiling water into it after it has emulsified.

are usually three or four chefs working in a team headed by their leader, the *chef de partie*, who are preparing and plating salads. The crew of the *garde manger* makes the dressings for the salads.

We serve the salad course—an important part of the romance of dining at sea—in the American style, just prior to the entrée. Whether the salad is simple, dramatic, or much-beloved—like the Holland America Line signature Salad Niçoise with Grilled Salmon and Honey Vinaigrette—the ingredients must be of the highest quality, the dressing must be distinctive, and the presentation must be lovely.

When making salad at home, seek out the best ingredients; for example, quality extra virgin olive oil. And rather than toss a salad in a bowl and serve it family style, see how fanciful and creative you can become with an individual plate presentation.

Find the romance of romaine; it's not hard, and you may never look at salads the same way again.

Garden Mixed Salad with Creamy Balsamic Caesar Dressing

To create a well-composed garden salad, your starting points should always include cool and crisp elements. From there you should focus on balancing flavor, texture, and appearance. Your end goal should be the enjoyment of pure freshness.

FOR THE DRESSING

In a blender, combine mayonnaise, balsamic vinegar, garlic, mustard, and anchovy paste. While blending, stream the extra virgin olive oil into the dressing through center of the lid. With a spatula, scrape out dressing into a nonreactive bowl. Season with salt and pepper. Cover and refrigerate until needed.

FOR THE SALAD

In a large bowl, toss all ingredients except chervil and Parmesan cheese. Add just enough reserved creamy balsamic Caesar dressing to lightly coat. Divide among plates and garnish with chervil. Using a vegetable peeler, shave curls of Parmesan atop each salad and serve.

YIELD: 6 SERVINGS

DRESSING

1 cup low-fat mayonnaise

¼ cup balsamic vinegar

½ teaspoon minced garlic

2 teaspoons Dijon mustard

1–2 teaspoons anchovy paste (from a tube)

¼ cup extra virgin olive oil

¼ teaspoon salt

¼ teaspoon freshly ground black pepper

SALAD

8 cups mixed baby greens (about 5 ounces)

Tender, pale inner leaves from 2 heads romaine

3 small tomatoes, diced

1 medium cucumber, peeled, halved, seeded, and thinly sliced

1 medium red onion, thinly sliced

2 tablespoons chopped fresh basil

1 bunch parsley, for garnish

1 (2½-ounce) piece Parmesan cheese

Salad Niçoise with Grilled Salmon and Honey Vinaigrette

VINAIGRETTE

¼ cup fresh lemon juice

4 tablespoons honey

½ tablespoon Dijon mustard

6 tablespoons extra virgin olive oil

½ tablespoon minced fresh garlic

½ tablespoon minced fresh tarragon

½ tablespoon minced fresh parsley

Salt

Freshly ground black pepper

SALAD AND SALMON

¼ pound haricots verts (thin green beans), ends trimmed

6 small tomatoes, quartered

½ cucumber, peeled, halved lengthwise, seeded, and diced

1 medium red bell pepper, cored, seeded, and sliced

6 scallions, white and tender green portions only, chopped

½ cup ripe olives (preferably Niçoise), pitted

4 (4-ounce) skinned salmon fillets (about 1-inch thick)

Salt

Freshly ground black pepper

2 tablespoons vegetable oil

1 tablespoon chopped fresh parsley

3 large hard-cooked eggs, quartered

1 (2-ounce) can anchovy fillets, drained and cut in half lengthwise

Fresh tarragon, for garnish

Here, the traditional Niçoise is made even more summery topped with grilled salmon. Pick up the other fresh ingredients at a farmers' market, and dinner becomes the catch of the day.

FOR THE VINAIGRETTE

In a nonreactive bowl, combine lemon juice, honey, and mustard. Slowly whisk in oil. Add garlic and herbs. Season with salt and pepper. Cover and refrigerate for up to 3 days until ready to use.

FOR THE SALAD

Prepare a bowl of ice water. Bring a medium saucepan of salted water to a boil. Add haricots verts and cook just until bright green and tender-crisp, about 3 minutes. Remove haricots verts with a strainer and set in ice water to stop the cooking. Drain and cut into ½-inch lengths.

In a large salad bowl, combine haricots verts, tomatoes, cucumber, bell pepper, scallions, and olives. Toss to combine; reserve.

FOR THE SALMON

Prepare grill. Season salmon with salt and pepper. Brush salmon with oil and grill on an oiled rack, set 5 to 6 inches above glowing coals (medium-high heat), just until opaque in center, about 4 minutes per side. Transfer salmon to a platter and keep warm.

TO SERVE

Toss salad mixture with parsley and enough vinaigrette to lightly coat. Divide among plates. Top each salad with a salmon fillet. Arrange eggs and anchovies attractively on salad. Garnish with basil and serve immediately.

> TIP | You can make a supermarket balsamic vinegar taste better by reducing it for a few minutes in a saucepan over medium heat. Let cool before using in a vinaigrette. —**Steve Kirsch**, director, culinary operation

Arugula and Frisée with Pear, Pancetta, Crottin de Chavignol, Pecans, and Fruit Vinaigrette

C rottin de Chavignol goat cheese becomes sharper and more pungent as it ages, so if you like flavor, choose one that is more yellow than white, with a light blue mold. With sweet pear, crispy nuts, salty pancetta, and bitter greens, there's no better match in the world!

FOR THE VINAIGRETTE

Cut passion fruit in half and scoop every bit of pulp from each half into a nonreactive sieve; press through all juice and pulp; discard seeds. In a nonreactive bowl, combine passion fruit pulp, lime juice, and sherry. Slowly whisk in olive oil. Season with salt and pepper. Cover and refrigerate until ready to use.

FOR THE SALAD

Combine arugula and frisée in bowl. Add half the pancetta and half the pecans. Toss with some reserved vinaigrette and divide among plates. Gently toss pear slices with a little vinaigrette and arrange on salads. Sprinkle salads with black pepper and remaining pancetta and pecans.

Place 2 slices goat cheese on the untoasted side of each baguette slice. Toast under the broiler or in a toaster oven until cheese warms. Top salads with baguette slices and serve immediately.

NOTE

If passion fruits are not available, you can order 30-ounce containers of The Perfect Puree's frozen passion fruit concentrate purée online.

YIELD: 4 SERVINGS

VINAIGRETTE

1 passion fruit (see Note)

Juice of 2 Key limes

1 tablespoon dry sherry

2 tablespoons extra virgin olive oil

Salt

Freshly ground black pepper

SALAD

2 cups arugula, washed, drained, and dried

2 cups frisée (curly endive), washed, drained, and dried

4 slices pancetta, diced and sautéed until crisp

1 cup pecan halves, toasted

2 Bartlett (or Williams) pears, peeled, cored, and sliced into $\frac{1}{16}$-inch slices

$\frac{1}{4}$ teaspoon freshly ground black pepper

2 Crottin de Chavignol goat cheeses, each sliced into 4 rounds

4 slices baguette, brushed with olive oil and toasted on one side

Warm Maine Lobster Salad with Asparagus and Pink Grapefruit

YIELD: 4 SERVINGS

½ cup kosher salt, plus extra for cooking vegetables

2 live 1½- to 2-pound Maine lobsters

12 spears green asparagus

12 spears white asparagus (see Note)

1 teaspoon sugar

1 tablespoon unsalted butter

2 pink grapefruits, segmented and juice reserved

2 tablespoons sherry vinegar

2 medium shallots, chopped

4 tablespoons extra virgin olive oil

Salt

Freshly ground black pepper

2 cups frisée lettuce

2 cups oak leaf lettuce

12 vine-ripened cherry tomatoes, halved

1 teaspoon deep-fried capers (see Note)

1 teaspoon cracked pink peppercorns

4 sprigs chervil

NOTE

White asparagus have a delicate flavor but tough peels. To remove peel, lie asparagus spear flat on cutting board and run peeler over it. Peel top to bottom but leave the buds (the last half inch or so) intact. And don't throw those peels away! Simmer them in chicken stock until tender, add cream, season, and purée in a blender for a delicious asparagus soup.

B ecause of lobster's exquisite flavor, texture, and healthfulness, it's a perfect salad companion. When you serve it on salad while still slightly warm, you can lap in the luxury of its intoxicating fragrance too.

FOR THE LOBSTERS

Unless you have a 4 to 6 gallon stockpot, fill 2 large pots with at least 1 gallon water each so the water fills the pots no more than three-quarters. Add ¼ cup kosher salt to each pot and bring to a rolling boil. Put 1 lobster in each pot and set timer for 12 minutes; when timer sounds, use tongs to remove lobsters from pots. Check for doneness by breaking lobsters in half where carapace meets tail and making sure tail meat is white and not translucent; return lobsters to pot if further cooking is necessary. Let cool at room temperature. Remove meat from claws and knuckles, trying to leave them whole. Break carcasses from tails and freeze carcasses for another use. Split tails in half lengthwise and remove meat. Remove intestines. Cover lobster meat with plastic wrap and refrigerate until ready to use.

FOR THE GREEN ASPARAGUS

Bring a saucepan of salted water to a boil. Prepare a large bowl of ice water. Pare away the fibrous outer layer of the asparagus, between ½ and a ⅓ of the lower stem portion. Lightly peel the remainder to just below the buds at the spear top. Place asparagus in the boiling water and cook until just crisp tender but still bright green, about 3 to 5 minutes. Remove asparagus with a strainer and set in ice water for 5 minutes to stop the cooking. Transfer to a clean kitchen towel to drain.

FOR THE WHITE ASPARAGUS

Cut the bottom ⅓ off the stems, peel the remaining two thirds from base of the stem, and then tie in a bundle with kitchen twine. Lie bundle in a pot and cover with water. Add 1 teaspoon salt, sugar, and butter. Bring to a simmer and cook gently for 5 minutes, so they're still crunchy. Turn off the heat and allow asparagus to cool inside liquid with a plate on top of them to keep them submerged. Once cool, remove from the pot and drain.

FOR THE VINAIGRETTE

In a blender, combine reserved grapefruit juice, half the grapefruit segments, vinegar, shallots, and olive oil; blend thoroughly. Season with salt and pepper. Cover and refrigerate until ready to use.

Prepare a steamer over simmering water. Cut asparagus into finger-lengths, dress with some vinaigrette, and arrange on plates. Toss lettuces and tomatoes with some vinaigrette and mound on asparagus. Lightly warm lobster tails and claws in steamer and divide among salads. Drizzle lobster with remaining vinaigrette and top with reserved grapefruit segments. Garnish with fried capers, pink peppercorns, and fresh chervil.

NOTE

To deep-fry capers, rinse, drain, and dry 2 tablespoons capers. Heat ¼ cup olive oil in small heavy skillet; fry capers, stirring, until slightly crisp and a shade darker, about 2 minutes. Transfer with a slotted spoon to paper towels to drain.

Master Chef Rudi's Salad with Mustard Cognac Dressing

Guaranteed to make heads turn and mouths gape, this bursting globe of colorful vegetables and lettuces is nothing short of stunning. The gourmet microgreens and exotic herbs listed below are only suggestions; it's best to simply stroll through your favorite produce shop or farmers' market and let your senses be your guide.

FOR THE SALAD

Wash all the ingredients very gently. Cut the tops from the tomatoes and hollow them out carefully, without breaking the tomato skin. Artfully arrange remaining salad ingredients in the tomatoes as if they are flowers in vases. Chill, loosely covered, in the refrigerator until ready to serve.

FOR THE MUSTARD COGNAC DRESSING

In a nonreactive bowl, combine shallot, vinegar, cognac, mustard, and sugar. Slowly whisk in olive oil. Season with salt and pepper.

TO SERVE

Place each salad on a plate and encircle it with some dressing. Serve extra dressing alongside.

YIELD: 6 SERVINGS

SALAD

6 large ripe but firm yellow or red tomatoes

1 small red bell pepper, thinly shaved

6 thin asparagus spears, quickly steamed and chilled

1 bunch frisée lettuce (use the yellow sprigs)

1 bunch baby oak leaf lettuce

1 bunch small akashiso leaves

1 bunch bulls blood beet tops

1 bunch magenta spinach

1 bunch baby tatsoi

1 bunch popcorn shoots

1 bunch mizuna lettuce

1 bunch enoki mushrooms

1 bunch baby red romaine lettuce

1 bunch chives

MUSTARD COGNAC DRESSING

1 medium shallot, finely chopped

6 tablespoons red wine vinegar

2 tablespoons cognac

2 tablespoons Dijon mustard

2 teaspoons sugar

$\frac{2}{3}$ cup extra virgin olive oil

Salt

Freshly ground black pepper

CHAPTER 6

PASTA & RISOTTO

Pasta is the original East-meets-West food, which makes it particularly appropriate for world travelers. In addition, everyone loves it in its infinite shapes, sizes, and variations. | On Holland America Line ships, making pasta is an art form. We at once want to be able to offer the familiar and the fanciful, and ideally, a dish that combines the best of both, such as our Holland America Line signature dish Ziti with Shellfish and Grilled Salmon in Pesto Sauce. | We not only want to satisfy our guests, but we also want to dazzle them, so pasta is handled very carefully and is always served at the proper texture and temperature. Each culinary team has a chef devoted exclusively to making perfect pasta every time. | Our behind-the-scenes orchestration of pasta has a few applications for the home

CUCUMBER LIME SMASH

Jonathan Bautista, bartender

Enjoy a new experience and try this cool and refreshing drink. It epitomizes the uniqueness of Holland America Line's signature cocktail program.

2 wedges lime, plus 1 extra for garnish
3 slices cucumber, with peel
1½ ounces vodka or gin
1½ ounces homemade sour mix (see Pantry Staples)

In a pint glass, hand-press lime wedges and 3 slices cucumber with a muddler. Fill glass with ice. Add vodka or gin and sour mix. Cap with shaker can and shake vigorously. Strain into a pint glass and garnish with lime slice on the rim.   YIELD: 1 DRINK

TINO DAAB
Executive chef

If you need to get the smell of onion or garlic off your hands, run them under cold water while rubbing with a stainless steel spoon—only stainless steel does the trick. We have no idea why it works, but it does. Try it!

cook. Our pasta cooks boil all pasta in batches to a toothsome al dente, tender but still firm. Then, the cook plunges the pasta into ice water to shock it. From there, the cook adds a little olive oil to keep it moist and stores it in individual portion containers until just prior to service.

When the order comes in from the waiter, the individual portion is then sautéed and given the appropriate saucing and presentation. Despite the fact that the pasta made on our ships is cooked in 50-gallon soup kettles, this pre-cooking technique is equally helpful for the busy home cook: boil up your pasta in the morning while having your coffee, make your sauce the night before, then presto, you have a tasty and easy-to-heat-up dinner.

Try different types of pasta. There are so many wonderful pasta products on the market, from fresh flavored pastas to a wide assortment of noodles in all shapes and sizes. And if you don't already have a risotto in your repertoire of pasta dishes, try this delicious Mushroom Risotto recipe.

For a change of pace, serve pasta as a more colorful alternative to potatoes or another starchy side dish. Pasta dishes offer stunning flavor, wonderful color, and dress up beautifully for either a side dish or main course.

Tagliatelle with Roasted Tomatoes, Garlic, and Olive Oil in Lemon Cream

This uncomplicated yet exquisite dish calls for a visit to a fresh pasta shop, or make your own pasta from your favorite recipe. You'll want a supple canvas to convey the sauce's delectable flavors.

FOR THE TOMATOES

Preheat oven to 425°F. Quarter tomatoes lengthwise, remove their seeds, and cut wedges in half. Gently toss in a bowl with 2 tablespoons olive oil, 1 teaspoon garlic, and basil. Place tomatoes on baking sheet. Roast until beginning to dry and wrinkle, about 20 minutes.

FOR THE SAUCE

In a large skillet, heat the remaining 2 tablespoons olive oil over medium heat. Add onion and remaining 1 teaspoon garlic and cook until translucent. Add wine and reduce by four-fifths. Add cream and reduce by one-half. Stir in lemon juice and horseradish. Season with salt, pepper, and sugar.

FOR THE PASTA

Cook pasta in a large pot of boiling salted water until tender but firm, 1 to 2 minutes for fresh, depending on thickness, or 9 to 12 minutes for dried. Drain and transfer to a large warmed serving bowl. Add sauce and toss. Divide among plates, drizzle with basil oil, and top with roasted tomatoes. Garnish with Parmesan shavings.

YIELD: 4 SERVINGS

4 ripe medium plum or Roma tomatoes

4 tablespoons olive oil

2 teaspoons minced fresh garlic

2 tablespoons very thinly sliced basil

1 small onion, finely chopped

1 cup dry white wine

1 cup heavy cream

Juice of 2 lemons

1 teaspoon prepared horseradish

Salt

Freshly ground black pepper

Pinch sugar

3 pounds fresh long, flat pasta, or 1 pound good-quality dried tagliatelle, preferably imported Italian

2 tablespoons basil oil, for garnish (see Pantry Staples)

Very thinly shaved Parmesan, for garnish

TIP | When cooking pasta, be sure you use enough water: at least one gallon of water for every pound of pasta; add 1 tablespoon of oil to keep the pasta from sticking to itself. —**Thomas Schumann**, executive chef

Mushroom Risotto

YIELD: 4 SERVINGS

½ stick (¼ cup) unsalted butter

½ pound fresh shiitake mushrooms, sliced

1 small onion, finely chopped

½ pound fresh button mushrooms, cleaned, trimmed, and cut into quarters

3 cups chicken stock, canned or homemade (see Pantry Staples)

½ pound arborio rice (about 1 cup plus 2 tablespoons)

¼ cup dry white wine

¼ cup finely grated Parmesan cheese

Salt

Freshly ground black pepper

2 tablespoons very thinly sliced basil

NOTE

Risotto is best served hot. And it should be firm, or al dente. If serving must be delayed, precook the risotto, but finish with the cheese and butter just prior to serving. You can also add chicken stock and more butter at that time, if needed.

The key to good risotto is how fast you cook it. If it cooks too quickly, the rice will look soft and lovely but have a hard center. Too slowly, and the texture will be too sticky. Taste as you go, and you'll do just fine.

Heat 1 tablespoon butter in a heavy skillet over medium-high heat. When foam subsides, add shiitake and sauté, stirring, until browned, about 5 minutes. Remove from heat; set aside (keep warm).

In a heavy casserole or enameled cast-iron pot, heat 1 tablespoon butter over medium-high heat. Add onion and cook, stirring, until softened, about 1 minute. Add 1 tablespoon butter to casserole and add button mushrooms; continue sautéing until any liquid they give off has evaporated, about 8 minutes.

Meanwhile, bring stock and 2 cups hot water to a simmer. Keep at a bare simmer, covered.

Add rice to onions and mushrooms, stirring so rice is coated with butter, about 1 minute. Add wine and simmer, stirring constantly, until absorbed. Stir in ½ cup simmering stock mixture and cook at a strong simmer, stirring frequently, until stock is absorbed. Continue simmering and adding stock ½ cup at a time, stirring frequently and letting each addition absorb before adding the next, until rice is tender but still firm and creamy (it should be the consistency of a thick soup), approximately 18 minutes. (There will be leftover stock.)

Stir in three-quarters of reserved shiitake. If necessary, thin risotto with a little more stock, stirring so rice absorbs all the liquid. Stir in Parmesan and the remaining 1 tablespoon butter. Season with salt and pepper. Garnish the top with remaining shiitake and basil and serve immediately.

> **TIP** To warm up a large serving bowl for pasta, place a colander in a bowl in the sink and drain your pasta into the colander. After a few seconds, the bowl will be heated and you can pour the water out and toss your pasta and sauce in the warm bowl. —**Tony Tudla**, executive chef

Ziti with Shellfish and Grilled Salmon in Pesto Sauce

It may seem like every component of this seafood extravaganza is cooking at the same time, but that's what happens when pasta meets seafood. Just have everything prepped before you begin and you'll be amazed how quickly it all comes together.

FOR THE CLAMS AND MUSSELS

In a medium stockpot, heat wine over medium heat. Add clams and mussels. Cover and steam for 2 minutes, shaking pot occasionally. Begin checking the shellfish; as soon as they open, transfer them to a colander placed over a bowl. Total steaming time will be about 4 minutes. Discard any clams or mussels that do not open. Strain shellfish broth—from both the cooking pot and the bowl—through a fine sieve lined with cheesecloth into a small bowl. Set shellfish and broth aside separately, keeping shellfish warm and moist until needed.

FOR THE SALMON

Preheat broiler. Season salmon with salt and pepper. Brush fillets with 2 tablespoons oil and broil just until opaque in center, about 4 minutes per side. Transfer salmon to a platter (keep warm).

FOR THE SHRIMP AND SCALLOP SAUCE

In a large skillet, heat remaining 2 tablespoons oil over medium heat. Add garlic and cook, stirring, until softened and translucent (do not brown). Add shrimp and scallops and cook, stirring, until just opaque; transfer to a large warmed serving bowl and keep warm. Add reserved shellfish broth to skillet and bring to a boil. Reduce heat and simmer, stirring, for 3 minutes. Add cream and reduce until sauce lightly coats the back of a spoon; adjust seasoning and keep warm.

FOR THE PASTA

Cook ziti in a stockpot of boiling salted water until tender but firm, 6 to 8 minutes. To serve, drain pasta and add it to shrimp and scallops in serving bowl. Pour reserved sauce over pasta and toss to coat. Divide pasta among individual plates. Top each mound of pasta with a salmon fillet and place clams and mussels still in their shells alongside. Garnish salmon and pasta with drops of pesto sauce, chopped tomato, and basil sprigs. Serve immediately.

YIELD: 8 SERVINGS

½ cup dry white wine

16 littleneck clams, scrubbed well under cold water

16 mussels, debearded and scrubbed well under cold water

8 (4-ounce) skinned salmon fillets (about 1-inch thick)

Salt

Freshly ground black pepper

4 tablespoons olive oil

1 tablespoon minced garlic

1 pound bay shrimp

1 pound bay scallops

½ cup heavy cream

1 pound dried ziti pasta

½ cup pesto sauce, store-bought or homemade (see Pantry Staples)

2 medium tomatoes, peeled, seeded, and diced (see Tip, page 86)

8 sprigs fresh basil

NOTE

As a variation, toss the pasta with 1 cup lobster bisque slowly reduced with 1 cup heavy cream and ¼ cup white wine.

Linguini with Rock Shrimp, Scallops, Tomatoes, and Baby Shrimp

YIELD: 4 SERVINGS

3 tablespoons olive oil, plus extra for drizzling

1 clove garlic, minced

½ cup diced onion

¼ cup chopped fresh thyme leaves

⅓ cup diced celery

⅓ cup diced carrot

⅓ cup diced leek, white part only

6 ripe medium tomatoes, peeled, seeded, and chopped coarsely (see Tip)

Salt

Freshly ground black pepper

1 pound dried thin linguini

½ pound rock shrimp, peeled and deveined

½ pound sea scallops

1 (6-ounce) package precooked frozen baby shrimp, thawed

¼ cup chopped fresh parsley

4 large sprigs basil

This fresh and flavorful pasta is easy enough for a weeknight, but looks and tastes as if you ordered it at some trendy restaurant. Don't forget to pick up the Merlot!

In a medium skillet, heat 1½ tablespoons oil over medium-high heat. Add garlic, onion, and thyme. Cook, stirring, until onion becomes softened and translucent. (Do not let onion brown.) Add celery, carrot, and leeks. Cook, stirring, until all the vegetables are softened. Add tomatoes and cook, stirring, for 15 minutes. Season with salt and pepper. Reserve and keep warm.

Meanwhile, cook linguini in a large pot of boiling salted water until tender but firm, 6 to 8 minutes. Drain and drizzle with a bit of olive oil to prevent sticking.

In a large skillet, heat the remaining 1½ tablespoons oil over high heat. Add rock shrimp and scallops. Cook, stirring, until shrimp turns pink, about 2 minutes. Add baby shrimp and heat through. Add reserved sauce and pasta and mix thoroughly. Divide linguini among plates. Sprinkle with parsley and garnish with basil sprigs. Serve immediately.

TIP | Recipes often call for tomatoes to be peeled and seeded before dicing or cooking them. The reason is looks (skins roll into little curls when they're cooked and they never break down) and taste (skins and especially seeds can be bitter). To skin and seed tomatoes, bring 1 quart water to a boil in a medium saucepan. With a paring knife, cut out the stems from the tomatoes and make a small "X" in the opposite ends. Plunge the tomatoes in the boiling water and leave them in just until the skins are loosened, 10 to 20 seconds. With a slotted spoon, transfer the tomatoes to a bowl of cold water to cool. Slip off the skins and cut the tomatoes in half along the equator. Gently but firmly squeeze the seeds from the halves. Now you're ready to chop or dice. For the most perfect dice, cut wedges from peeled tomatoes, remove all inner flesh, pulp, and seeds, square off remaining tomato shell, and cut into perfect dice. —**Guido Scarpellino,** corporate culinary trainer

Penne with Sausage, Mozzarella, Tomatoes, and Basil, with Chunky Marinara Sauce

Here's a comfort food classic with much more pizzazz than the usual mac 'n' cheese. Don't forget to buy extra mini mozzarella balls for the kids!

FOR THE MARINARA SAUCE

In a heavy, medium saucepan over moderate heat, heat olive oil until shimmering. Add onions and garlic, cover, and cook over low heat, stirring occasionally, until softened and translucent, about 10 minutes. Add tomato purée, canned tomatoes with their juice (smash them with a spoon as you add them to the pan), and parsley. Simmer, uncovered, for 30 minutes.

Pass the sauce through a food mill or fine-mesh sieve to remove the solids. Return sauce to saucepan and simmer over low heat until very thick (there will be about 2 cups). Add fresh tomatoes and cook for 2 minutes more. Add salt, pepper, and basil; reserve.

FOR THE PASTA

Cook penne in a large pot of boiling salted water until tender but firm, 6 to 8 minutes. Drain and transfer to a large warmed serving bowl. Drizzle with a bit of olive oil to prevent sticking.

While the pasta cooks, in a large skillet, heat olive oil over medium-high heat. Add garlic and yellow bell peppers and sauté until peppers are softened. Add cherry tomatoes and half the cooked sausage and sauté for about 1 minute more. Pour in 1 pint reserved tomato sauce (save remainder for another use or freeze).

Pour sauce over reserved penne, add half the Pecorino Romano cheese, and toss to coat. Season with salt, pepper, and pepper flakes. Lightly toss in mozzarella balls and chopped basil.

In a skillet, reheat remaining cooked sausage slices and sautéed onions. Divide sauced penne among plates and top with reheated sausage and onions. Garnish with remaining Pecorino slices and whole basil leaves.

> **TIP** If your homemade pasta sauce tastes a little sharp, instead of adding sugar, try adding a little butter right before you toss it with the pasta. It will help round out the flavors considerably. —**Peter Kofler**, executive chef

---

YIELD: 4 SERVINGS

MARINARA SAUCE

2 tablespoons olive oil

3 medium onions, thinly sliced

4 large cloves garlic, finely chopped

½ cup canned tomato purée

1 can (16 ounces) Italian plum tomatoes and their juice

5 sprigs parsley

12 fresh plum tomatoes (about 1½ pounds), peeled, seeded, and coarsely chopped (see Tip, page 86)

½ teaspoon salt

¼ teaspoon freshly ground black pepper

2 tablespoons minced fresh basil

PASTA

1 pound dried penne pasta

½ cup olive oil, plus extra for drizzling pasta

2 tablespoons minced fresh garlic

1 large yellow bell pepper, cored and cut into thin strips

1 pound cherry tomatoes

½ pound Italian sausage, cooked and sliced

½ pound Pecorino Romano cheese, shaved

Salt

Freshly ground black pepper

Crushed red pepper flakes

¼ pound fresh mini mozzarella balls

1 bunch fresh basil, half chopped and half left whole for garnish

¼ pound onions, sliced and sautéed

CHAPTER 7

FISH & SHELLFISH

There are plenty of fish in the sea, and where better to enjoy them then sailing on the ocean? So great is the synergy between an ocean-going ship and the fruits of the sea that a meal of seafood becomes a unique celebration of the journey itself. | The culinary team at Holland America works with over thirty-five species of fish when creating our menus and developing recipes. The fishmonger aboard our ships selects the freshest seafood of unquestionable origin. | Our commitment to the origin of ingredients is shown and celebrated in our signature program Alaska Goes Wild for Alaska Salmon; we will only serve Alaska salmon on our Alaska cruises. On our European itineraries, however, the fishmongers purchase Norwegian salmon. | It's also important

GRAPEFRUIT COSMOPOLITAN

Rogelio Camposano, bartender

One of the world's most fashionable libations, with many variations. No matter the style, Holland America Line makes all of its house Cosmos with premium vodkas, fresh citrus, and cranberry juice.

2 wedges lime

⅛ of a pink grapefruit

1½ ounces vodka

1½ ounces homemade sour mix (see Pantry Staples)

1 ounce cranberry juice cocktail

1 long zest of fresh grapefruit

In a pint glass, hand-press lime wedges and grapefruit with a muddler. Fill glass with ice. Add vodka, sour mix, and cranberry juice. Cap with shaker can and shake vigorously. Strain into a chilled martini glass and garnish with a grapefruit twist across the rim.

YIELD: 1 DRINK

THOMAS KRIEGER
Executive chef

Fish is cooked when the flesh has turned from translucent to opaque and springs back lightly when touched. The flesh should still be juicy. If you wait until "fish flakes easily with a fork," as some recipes mistakenly suggest, your fish will be overcooked.

CHEF'S NOTE FROM THE GALLEY

to know that Holland America Line does not use endangered species—we want to keep the oceans safe and bountiful. And speaking of safety, in addition to using the freshest fish, we have impeccable seafood culinary practices and protocols, including storage coolers and rooms devoted solely to the care and initial preparation of all our seafood.

The recipes in this chapter will appeal to people who frequently cook fish as well as novices, and will be relished by all who taste the dishes. Each recipe specifies the size and weight for the requisite fish and gives the cooking time; right there, the trickiest element of cooking fish is made simple. You'll notice that all of these dishes are served with some kind of potato. It's a little trick: when presenting fish, I always prefer to lay it on starches or potatoes, to give it some height.

If you are inexperienced with cooking fish, first try our Balsamic Maple Glazed Salmon with Steamed Spinach and Sautéed Cherry Tomatoes—it's one of those perennial favorites on Holland America Line menus. For additional great fish recipes, please see chapter 3.

Cedar-Planked Halibut with Alaskan King Crab and Béarnaise Sauce

Guests rave about this Northwest-inspired dish, developed as part of Holland America Line's Signature of Excellence initiative. Plank cooking imparts a subtle smoky flavor, which provides an intriguing counterpoint to the elegant crab topping.

Place cedar plank in sink and cover with water, weighing it down with a can or small pot to keep it submerged. Let soak about 1 hour. Preheat oven to 425°F. Drain cedar plank and place in oven for 10 minutes. The plank will begin to crack and smoke (this is normal).

Season halibut fillets with salt and pepper and sprinkle with thyme. Place halibut directly onto cedar plank and roast until fish is just opaque in center, 10 to 15 minutes. Remove plank from oven and remove halibut from plank.

To serve, heat butter in a small heavy skillet over moderate heat until foam subsides. Add crab meat and claws and heat through, stirring gently, about 2 minutes. Top halibut with crab meat and garnish with crab claws and asparagus. Spoon some sauce over the fish and crabmeat and serve the remaining sauce separately. Garnish with thyme.

YIELD: 4 SERVINGS

1 untreated red cedar plank, approximately 8 inches x 12 inches (see Note)

4 (6-ounce) skinless halibut fillets, each about 1¼ inches thick

Salt

Freshly ground black pepper

2 teaspoons finely minced thyme leaves

1 tablespoon unsalted butter

½ pound fully cooked Alaskan king crab meat, picked clean of any shell fragments

4 cooked crab claws

8 asparagus spears, steamed

Béarnaise Sauce (see Pantry Staples)

Fresh thyme leaves, for garnish

NOTE

Cedar planks are readily available in packages from kitchen stores, or can be cut to your specifications at home centers. Buy ¾-inch-thick untreated cedar at your local home center and have it cut to fit inside of a pan that is 13 inches x 9 inches; the pan will catch any drips while cooking. Soaked planks that are 1 inch thick can also be used directly on your outdoor grill.

Balsamic Maple Glazed Salmon with Steamed Spinach and Sautéed Cherry Tomatoes

YIELD: 4 SERVINGS

¼ cup orange juice

¼ cup maple syrup

5 tablespoons balsamic vinegar

4 teaspoons finely minced garlic

3 tablespoons olive oil

4 (1-inch-thick) salmon steaks or fillets (about 6 ounces each)

Salt

Freshly ground black pepper

1 (10-ounce) bag dark, crinkly-leaf spinach, well washed

1 cup yellow grape tomatoes

1 cup halved cherry tomatoes

Mashed potatoes (optional; see Side Dishes)

Healthful, flavorful, and colorful—this recipe has everything you're looking for in a salmon dish. Serve on a bed of mashed potatoes to satisfy more hearty appetites.

In a small saucepan, combine orange juice, maple syrup, 3 tablespoons balsamic vinegar, and 2 teaspoons garlic. Bring to a boil and cook for 5 to 6 minutes. Stir in 1 tablespoon oil.

Prepare grill. Season salmon with salt and pepper. Brush salmon generously with glaze and grill on an oiled rack set 5 to 6 inches above glowing coals (medium-high heat) until just cooked through, about 5 minutes on each side (do not allow it to burn).

Meanwhile, place spinach in a 4-quart saucepan over medium heat. Cover and let steam with just the water clinging to the leaves, stirring once, until wilted. Season with salt and pepper and set aside.

Heat remaining 2 tablespoons olive oil in heavy medium skillet over medium-high heat. Add tomatoes and remaining 2 teaspoons garlic to skillet; sauté 1 minute. Add remaining 2 tablespoons balsamic vinegar; sauté 30 seconds. Season with salt and pepper.

TO SERVE

Place mashed potatoes (if using) on plate. Top with salmon fillet. Top salmon with some spinach. Spoon tomatoes alongside salmon and serve immediately.

TIP | To store fresh fish, first wrap it in high-quality, unwaxed butcher paper, which keeps moisture away from the flesh. Then place the package in a plastic bag to prevent oxidation from air exposure, which can turn the flesh gray and dull. —**Markus Jenni**, executive chef

Apricot Glazed Salmon with Soy, Garlic, and Ginger and Baby Vegetables

S weet and hot, this unusual salmon glaze works wonderfully on chicken or even tofu, too. Choose colorful baby vegetables that complement the fish's glistening orange hues.

FOR THE BABY VEGETABLES

Fill an 8-quart stockpot with water and set it over high heat. When the water boils, salt it well, then add the desired baby vegetables. Simmer until vegetables are tender but still a bit crisp, checking them individually as certain types will cook faster than others. Use a slotted spoon to transfer vegetables to a platter as they become tender.

FOR THE GLAZE

Preheat oven to 450°F. Line bottom of a broiler pan with foil, then grease rack of pan. In a saucepan over medium heat, combine apricot nectar, dried apricots, honey, soy sauce, ginger, 2 teaspoons garlic, cinnamon, and cayenne. Bring to a boil, then reduce heat to medium-low and simmer, stirring occasionally, for about 20 minutes, or until reduced by about half. Do not allow to burn. Remove ¼ cup of the glaze for basting and set the remainder aside.

FOR THE SALMON

Arrange salmon fillets on rack of broiling pan; pat dry. Brush with glaze for basting. Let stand for 5 minutes, then brush with more glaze. Roast salmon in middle of oven for 10 minutes. Turn on broiler and brush salmon with glaze again. Broil 4 to 5 inches from the heat until interior flesh has just turned opaque but is still juicy, 3 to 5 minutes. Do not allow to burn.

TO SERVE

In a medium saucepan, heat butter over medium-low heat. Add remaining 1 teaspoon garlic and baby vegetables. Cook, stirring gently, until vegetables are heated through. Sprinkle with coarse salt and season with pepper. Divide salmon among plates and place baby vegetables alongside. Serve with reserved glaze and savory rice, if desired.

NOTE

Kohlrabi are bulbous green vegetables, sometimes with purple streaks, that taste similar to a mild turnip. They, and the other baby vegetables listed, are available seasonally at specialty produce markets.

YIELD: 4 SERVINGS

BABY VEGETABLES

Your choice of:

4 baby turnips, trimmed and quartered lengthwise

8 baby carrots (not from a bag), peeled, keeping ½ inch of stem intact, and halved lengthwise if large

4 baby pattypan squash, halved

8 ounces baby zucchini, ends trimmed, halved

4 pencil-thin asparagus, trimmed

4 small kohlrabi (see Note)

GLAZE AND SALMON

1½ cups apricot nectar

⅓ cup chopped dried apricots

2 tablespoons honey

2 tablespoons reduced sodium soy sauce

1 tablespoon grated fresh ginger

3 teaspoons minced garlic

¼ teaspoon ground cinnamon

⅛ teaspoon cayenne pepper

1½ pounds skinless center-cut salmon fillet (1½ inches thick), cut into 4 pieces

2 tablespoons unsalted butter

Coarse salt

Freshly ground black pepper

Savory Golden Rice (optional; see Side Dishes)

Peppercorn Crusted Monkfish on Braised Fingerling Potatoes with a Mustard Vinaigrette

MUSTARD VINAIGRETTE

2 tablespoons extra virgin olive oil

⅓ cup puréed caramelized onions (see Note)

1 tablespoon sherry

2 tablespoons whole-grain mustard

Salt

Freshly ground black pepper

MUSHROOMS, POTATOES, AND BABY VEGETABLES

¾ pound fresh chanterelles

2 tablespoons finely minced shallot

2 tablespoons olive oil

1 tablespoon unsalted butter, melted

½ teaspoon coarse sea salt

2 tablespoons dry white wine

1 teaspoon fresh lemon juice

2 cups fingerling or baby red bliss potatoes, washed and halved lengthwise

1 cup vegetable stock, canned or homemade (see Pantry Staples)

1 sprig thyme

2 very small fennel bulbs, halved lengthwise

8 baby carrots, trimmed

MONKFISH

4 (4-ounce) monkfish fillets, center cut

⅛ cup coarsely ground mixed peppercorns (pink, green, black, and white) mixed with ⅛ cup flour

Coarse salt

1 tablespoon unsalted butter

1 tablespoon olive oil

A fabulous fall fish dish, with its harvest-time potatoes and mushrooms and peppery, mustardy flavors. Cod fillets work equally well.

FOR THE MUSTARD VINAIGRETTE

Warm olive oil in a pan and whisk in caramelized onion purée. Add sherry to thin slightly and then add mustard. Season to taste; the consistency should coat the back of a wooden spoon.

FOR THE MUSHROOMS

Cut chanterelles in half. In a medium bowl, whisk 1 tablespoon shallot, 1 tablespoon oil, ½ tablespoon butter, and ¼ teaspoon salt. Add mushrooms and toss to coat. In a large nonstick skillet, add mushrooms and sauté, stirring, until barely tender, about 2 minutes. Add wine and cook, stirring, until liquid is evaporated and mushrooms are tender, about 5 minutes. Transfer to a bowl and toss with lemon juice; set aside (keep warm).

FOR THE POTATOES AND BABY VEGETABLES

In a medium bowl, whisk the remaining 1 tablespoon shallot, 1 tablespoon oil, ½ tablespoon butter, and ¼ teaspoon salt. Add potatoes and toss to coat. Wipe out mushroom skillet and return to medium heat. Add potatoes and sauté for 3 minutes. Add vegetable stock and thyme and cook very gently until potatoes are tender; set aside. Bring a large pot of salted water to a boil and drop in baby fennel bulbs and baby carrots. Return to a boil and cook until both are tender; drain and set aside.

FOR THE MONKFISH

Dredge monkfish in flour and peppercorn mixture. Season with salt. In a heavy skillet, heat butter and oil. Add fish and cook until just opaque in center, about 4 minutes per side. To serve, arrange potatoes on plates. Top potatoes with fish. Surround fish with baby vegetables and mushrooms. Drizzle fish and plate with vinaigrette and serve.

NOTE

To make caramelized onion purée, heat 2 tablespoons olive oil in a large skillet over medium heat. Add 2 large onions thinly sliced and salt and ground white pepper. Cook until onions begin to brown, stirring frequently, about 8 minutes. Add ½ cup chicken broth and reduce heat; simmer until liquid is almost completely evaporated. Let cool slightly, scrape into a blender, and purée.

Seared Cajun Tuna Steak with Plum Tomato Confit, Horseradish Roesti, and Basil Oil

T he combination of smooth and crispy textures, spicy heat, and sweet confit will awaken your palate, bite after delightful bite.

YIELD: 4 SERVINGS

FOR THE TOMATOES

Preheat oven to 300°F. Oil a large rimmed baking sheet. Arrange tomatoes on baking sheet. Scatter thyme sprigs and garlic cloves on top. Drizzle with olive oil, then sprinkle with coarse sea salt. Bake tomatoes 45 minutes. Turn tomatoes over; continue to bake until tomatoes shrink slightly but are still plump and moist, about 1 hour longer. Cool completely. Peel off skins. (Can be prepared 1 day ahead. Cover and refrigerate. Bring to room temperature before using.)

FOR THE HORSERADISH ROESTI

Mound potatoes in a kitchen towel and squeeze out as much liquid as possible. In a large mixing bowl, combine potatoes with horseradish and oil; season with salt and pepper.

Preheat oven to 200°F. Put a baking sheet in the oven and place a rack on it. In a 10-inch nonstick skillet, heat 2 tablespoons butter over medium heat. Spread potato mixture into a layer in the pan. Brown until golden and crusty on the bottom, 5 to 7 minutes. Invert roesti onto pan lid and remove pan from heat. Add remaining 2 tablespoons butter to preheated pan. Slide roesti into pan raw side down and brown for an additional 5 to 7 minutes. Transfer roesti to cutting board. With a 3½-inch round cutter, cut out 4 rounds from the roesti. Place rounds on rack in oven to keep warm.

FOR THE CAJUN TUNA

Rub each tuna steak with 1½ teaspoon oil and Cajun seasoning. In a cast-iron skillet, heat remaining 2 tablespoons oil until it begins to smoke. Sear tuna on each side for only 1 minute—the tuna is served rare. Transfer to cutting board and cut each steak into 2 triangles. Stand 2 triangles on each plate with a roesti and spoonful of tomato confit. Decorate plate with dots of basil oil and crème fraîche.

TOMATOES

2½ pounds large plum tomatoes, quartered lengthwise and seeds and membranes removed

4 large fresh thyme sprigs

3 cloves garlic, unpeeled

¼ cup olive oil

1 teaspoon coarse sea salt

HORSERADISH ROESTI

1 pound Yukon gold potatoes, chilled and shredded

¼ cup coarsely grated peeled fresh horseradish or 1 tablespoon prepared horseradish

4 teaspoons vegetable oil

Kosher salt

Freshly ground black pepper

4 tablespoons unsalted butter

CAJUN TUNA

4 (6-ounce) tuna steaks, each about 1 inch thick

¼ cup peanut or canola oil

2 tablespoons Cajun seasoning (see Note)

Basil oil, for garnish (see Pantry Staples)

Crème fraîche, for garnish (see Pantry Staples)

NOTE

For homemade Cajun seasoning, in a small bowl blend the following: ½ teaspoon salt, 1 teaspoon minced fresh thyme, ½ teaspoon dried oregano, ½ teaspoon cayenne pepper (or to taste), ½ teaspoon sweet paprika, ½ teaspoon ground black pepper, and ½ teaspoon fennel seeds, crushed.

CHAPTER 8

POULTRY

One of the most difficult aspects of putting this book together was narrowing down the recipes to be included—there are so many Holland America Line signature dishes that have become oft-requested favorites of our guests and so many that deserve to become new favorites for the home cook. | When it comes to poultry preparation on our ships, each chef is dedicated to preparing one type of poultry—farm-raised chicken, duck, turkey, pheasant, or quail—in an array of preparations. One chef will only cook chicken for the entire week; he or she is specially trained in our Holland America Line signature chicken preparations. Likewise with turkey and other types of birds. | At Holland America Line we pride ourselves on our

CORAL DROP

Rodolfo Sio, bartender

One of four exciting flavors of Lemon Drop served by Holland America Line, the Coral Drop has a hue reminiscent of some of the most exotic marine animals of the sea.

2 wedges lemon, plus 1 extra wedge for garnish
1½ ounces mandarin-orange flavored vodka
⅛ ounce black raspberry liqueur, such as Chambord
1½ ounces homemade sour mix (see Pantry Staples)
Sugar, for rim

In a pint glass, hand-press 2 lemon wedges with a muddler. Fill glass with ice. Add vodka, black raspberry liqueur, and sour mix. Cap with shaker can and shake vigorously. Strain into a chilled martini glass with a sugared half rim. Garnish with remaining lemon wedge.   YIELD: 1 DRINK

FRANZ SCHAUNIG
Executive chef

The best way to skin a chicken: Use a paper towel to grab the chicken parts and pull off the skin. The paper towel will give you a good grip and is especially useful for removing skin from the chicken legs, which can be particularly tough.

CHEF'S NOTE FROM THE GALLEY

spirit of exploration, expansion, and evolution. Our menus encompass an expanding universe of culinary possibilities, incorporating globally inspired foods like *Soto Ayam*, a typical Indonesian dish, which began as one of the most popular meals of our crew and evolved into a Holland America Line signature dish.

Also in the realm of exploration, there is a recipe for pheasant, which is not often used by the home chef. We offer pheasant on all our Alaska cruises—a heartwarming treat when it's cool outside. But here is the secret of this chapter: you can substitute one poultry for another in all of these recipes. Use the same techniques for chicken as you would for the pheasant meat in the Roasted Pheasant with Sweet Potato Purée, Sautéed Cabbage, and Cranberry Compote, and *voila*!

Use turkey instead of chicken in the stir-fry, or replace the turkey breast with a chicken breast in the Parmesan Crusted Turkey Tenderloin with Honey Mustard Sauce. It's about inspiration and exploration.

Stir-Fried Chicken with Peanuts

An easy and flavorful dish, with silky chicken and mushrooms, and colorful, crunchy vegetables.

In a large skillet or wok, heat 1 tablespoon oil. When smoking, add chicken and stir-fry lightly, until cooked through. With a slotted spoon, remove chicken and reserve (keep warm).

Add remaining 1 tablespoon oil to wok and stir-fry onion, carrot, celery, bell pepper, snow peas, and mushrooms for 2 minutes. Add water chestnuts. In a small bowl, whisk together chicken stock, vinegar, soy sauce, hoisin sauce, garlic, ginger, sugar, and cornstarch; add to vegetable mixture and bring to a boil.

Remove vegetable mixture from heat and stir in chicken. Divide between plates and sprinkle with scallions and peanuts. Serve immediately with steamed rice.

YIELD: 2 SERVINGS

2 tablespoons peanut oil

½ pound boneless, skinless chicken breast or thigh meat, sliced thinly

1 small onion, halved and sliced

1 medium carrot, peeled and thinly sliced

1 stalk celery, sliced

½ medium red bell pepper, very thinly sliced

½ cup snow peas, cut in half lengthwise

6 fresh shiitake mushrooms, stems removed and caps sliced

¼ cup sliced water chestnuts

½ cup chicken stock, canned or homemade (see Pantry Staples)

1 tablespoon rice wine vinegar

1 tablespoon soy sauce

1 teaspoon hoisin sauce

1 teaspoon minced garlic

½ teaspoon minced fresh ginger

1 teaspoon sugar

1 tablespoon cornstarch or arrowroot

2 scallions, trimmed and thinly sliced

2 tablespoons chopped dry-roasted peanuts

Steamed rice

NOTE

A delightful garnish for many Asian dishes is *krupuk* (pictured), a prawn cracker. They can be purchased in dried form at Asian grocery stores.

Poached Lemon Infused Chicken Breast with Orange Orzo and Sliced Squash

T he chicken in this light and refreshing preparation is poached to allow the various citrus flavors to shine through.

Remove skin and trim wing bone from chicken breasts; reserve. In a stockpot, combine stock, wine, lemon juice, lemon grass, bay leaf, and peppercorns. Bring to a light simmer. Season chicken with salt and pepper and place in the simmering stock. Return to a simmer and poach until cooked through, about 10 minutes. Remove chicken, place on a platter, and tent with foil to keep warm. Reserve poaching liquid at a slow simmer.

In a 2-quart saucepan, heat olive oil over medium heat. Add shallots and cook until softened. Add orzo, stirring to coat with the oil, and then add 2 cups reserved poaching liquid, orange juice, and half the orange zest. Bring to a simmer and cook orzo, stirring occasionally, until liquid is absorbed, about 12 minutes. Keep warm.

Meanwhile, in a small saucepan, heat butter over medium heat. Add sugar and cook until golden brown. Add half of the orange segments, stir once, and remove pan from heat to allow segments to soften in syrup.

Add water to remaining simmering stock to equal 2 cups; season with salt. Add zucchini and squash and cook, covered, until tender. Remove with a slotted spoon to a warm bowl and ladle a little poaching liquid over them to keep them warm.

To serve, return chicken breasts to simmering poaching liquid just long enough to reheat. Stir parsley, chopped basil, and the remaining orange segments into the orzo and divide it among the plates. Place a breast on each pile of orzo. With a slotted spoon, transfer squash slices to plates. Garnish plates with caramelized orange segments, remaining reserved orange peel, and whole thyme leaves. Serve immediately.

NOTE

For this recipe, seek out chicken with the best flavor and texture, which may mean free-range, organic, or corn-fed.

YIELD: 4 SERVINGS

4 chicken breasts (see Note)

2 cups chicken stock, canned or homemade (see Pantry Staples)

1 cup white wine, preferably Chardonnay

Juice of 1 lemon

1 stalk lemon grass, split and crushed

1 bay leaf

10 white peppercorns

Salt

Freshly ground black pepper

2 tablespoons olive oil

1 tablespoon minced shallots

1 cup orzo pasta

2 oranges, peel removed and very thinly sliced, flesh segmented, and peel, segments, and juice separately reserved

1 tablespoon unsalted butter

1 tablespoon light brown sugar

1 small green zucchini, sliced diagonally

1 small yellow summer squash, sliced diagonally

1 tablespoon chopped Italian parsley

1 tablespoon chopped fresh thyme, plus 4 whole leaves for garnish

Roasted Pheasant with Sweet Potato Purée, Sautéed Cabbage, and Cranberry Compote

YIELD: 4 SERVINGS

CRANBERRY COMPOTE

Grated zest from 2 oranges

2 cups fresh orange juice

1 cup sugar

1 cinnamon stick

1 pound fresh or frozen cranberries

SWEET POTATO PURÉE

2 large sweet potatoes, peeled and cut into 1-inch pieces

1 cup milk

1 cinnamon stick

3 strips zest from 1 orange, with juice from orange squeezed and reserved separately

1½ teaspoons unsalted butter

½ apple, diced

½ banana, sliced

1 tablespoon sugar

½ cup heavy cream

Salt

SAUTÉED CABBAGE

¼ pound bacon, chopped

1 tablespoon unsalted butter

1 small head Savoy cabbage, shredded

Salt

Freshly ground black pepper

At once elegant and hearty, this phenomenal pheasant adds sparkle to the fall and winter season. Every component of the dish features an abundance of the flavors and ingredients we celebrate during the cooler months.

FOR THE CRANBERRY COMPOTE

In a medium, nonreactive saucepan, combine orange zest, orange juice, sugar, and cinnamon stick. Bring to a boil over medium heat. Add cranberries and cook, stirring occasionally, until berries just pop, 10 to 12 minutes. Let cool and transfer to a small, nonreactive bowl; cover and set aside. (Cranberry compote may be kept chilled, covered, for up to 3 days.)

FOR THE SWEET POTATO PURÉE

In a large saucepan, combine sweet potatoes, milk, cinnamon stick, and orange zest. Add water to cover. Bring to a boil over high heat. Reduce heat and simmer until sweet potato is tender, about 15 minutes. Drain in a colander, reserving sweet potato and orange peels.

In that same saucepan, heat butter over medium heat. Add reserved orange peels, apple, and banana. Sauté for 3 minutes. Add sugar and reserved orange juice and cook, stirring, until fruit begins to brown or caramelize. With a slotted spoon, transfer fruit to the bowl of a food processor. Add cream to the orange zest in saucepan and cook, scraping the bottom of the pot, for 1 minute more. Remove pan from the heat and discard orange zest. Strain cream into the bowl of the food processor.

Add drained sweet potatoes to the cream and fruit in the food processor and purée until smooth. Season with salt. Transfer purée to the top of a double boiler, cover, and keep warm.

FOR THE SAUTÉED CABBAGE

In a large heavy skillet, cook bacon over medium heat until crisped. Remove with slotted spoon and drain on paper towels. Add butter to bacon fat in skillet and heat over medium-high heat. Toss in cabbage and cook quickly over high heat for about 5 minutes or until tender but still crisp. Stir in bacon pieces. Season with salt and pepper; keep warm.

FOR THE PHEASANT

Preheat oven to 450°F. Season pheasants inside and out with salt and pepper. Truss each bird: use kitchen string to tie the legs together, pressing the legs close to the pheasant body, then turn the bird over and fold its wings back behind it. Coat each bird with 1 tablespoon butter. Roast them breast side up in a large roasting pan for 15 minutes, or until medium-rare. (It is important to not overcook the pheasants, as they are very lean birds.) Remove from oven, tent with foil, and let rest for 15 minutes. Remove breasts and thighs and bone them, reserving bones, carcass, legs, and any degreased juices to make sauce. Tent breasts and thighs with foil to keep warm.

FOR THE GAME SAUCE

In a large heavy saucepan, heat remaining 2 tablespoons butter over medium heat. Add reserved pheasant bones and shallots and cook, stirring, until shallots are slightly browned, about 15 minutes. Add brandy and cook, scraping the bottom of the pan, until liquid is almost evaporated. Add juniper berries, orange zest, orange juice, black pepper, wine, and veal stock; bring to a boil. Reduce heat and simmer until sauce coats the back of a spoon. Strain through a fine sieve into a small saucepan. Season with salt and pepper. Reserve and keep warm.

TO SERVE

If necessary, reheat reserved pheasant breasts and thighs in the oven until an instant-read thermometer inserted into the thickest part of the breast registers 160°F; let rest 10 minutes tented with foil. Meanwhile, spoon some sweet potato purée on each plate. Place some cabbage in the center. Top cabbage with a pheasant thigh. Partially slice breast and place on thigh. Spoon some sauce and cranberries over breast meat and serve.

NOTE

Pheasant is available at specialty butcher shops. Call in advance to order. Wild pheasants are usually smaller birds, and thus will cook in less time. If you are using wild pheasants, please adjust the recipe accordingly. If you wish to substitute chicken, choose one 5 to 6 pound bird and roast for 45 minutes to an hour until an instant-read thermometer inserted into the center of the breast registers 155°F.

TIP Lightly basting a roasting chicken with a mixture of 3 tablespoons dark corn syrup and 4 tablespoons butter will ensure a well-browned bird. —**Christian Carbillet**, executive chef

PHEASANT AND GAME SAUCE

2 farm-raised pheasants (2½ to 3 pounds each), innards removed and wing tips and necks trimmed (see Note)

Salt

Freshly ground black pepper

4 tablespoons unsalted butter, softened

½ cup chopped shallots

1 cup brandy

1 teaspoon juniper berries

Grated zest of 1 orange

1 cup fresh orange juice

1 teaspoon cracked black peppercorns

1 quart dry red wine

1 quart veal stock (see Pantry Staples)

Parmesan Crusted Turkey Tenderloin with Honey Mustard Sauce

YIELD: 4 SERVINGS

TURKEY

6 tablespoons unsalted butter, melted

1 teaspoon minced fresh garlic

1 teaspoon chopped thyme

⅓ cup plus 1 tablespoon Dijon mustard

½ cup plus 2 tablespoons panko (Japanese breadcrumbs, see Note page 48) or fresh breadcrumbs

½ cup grated Parmesan cheese

2 teaspoons finely minced fresh parsley

4 (6-ounce) turkey tenderloins

HONEY MUSTARD SAUCE

¼ cup red wine vinegar

½ cup whole-grain Dijon mustard

½ cup mayonnaise

¼ cup sour cream

2 tablespoons honey

½ teaspoon minced fresh garlic

TO ASSEMBLE

2 tablespoons peanut or canola oil

Vegetable Risotto, optional (see Side Dishes)

16 cherry tomatoes, sautéed in olive oil and salt until ready to burst, for garnish

---

Here's a crunchy turkey tender with a creamy sweet mustard sauce. What's not to like? Pounded chicken breasts work equally well.

FOR THE TURKEY

Melt butter in a small saucepan over low heat. Add garlic and thyme and cook very gently for 1 to 3 minutes. Whisk in mustard. Remove from heat and let cool enough to touch but not to solidify. Whip vigorously until mixture thickens and becomes smooth and creamy (mixture shouldn't separate). Reserve.

Combine panko, Parmesan, and parsley and put on a plate. Dip tenderloins in reserved Dijon marinade covering all surfaces. Dredge well with Parmesan mixture. Place turkey on baking sheets, a few inches apart, so they are not touching. Cover with plastic wrap and refrigerate a minimum of 2 hours, or up to overnight, to set breading.

FOR THE HONEY MUSTARD SAUCE

In a small saucepan, reduce red wine vinegar over low heat until almost evaporated; set aside. In a small bowl, whisk all remaining ingredients together well. Add vinegar reduction and thoroughly combine.

TO ASSEMBLE AND SERVE

Heat oven to 375°F. Heat oil in a large heavy skillet over medium-high heat. Sauté turkey in batches (if necessary) until crust is deep golden, about 4 minutes per side. Transfer to a baking sheet to finish in the oven, about 8 to 10 minutes. To serve, cut tenderloins in half on the diagonal and spoon vegetable risotto, if using, alongside. Garnish with cherry tomatoes and drizzle plate with honey mustard sauce.

> **TIP** The U.S. Department of Agriculture and other food agencies in the world have concluded that washing poultry before cooking will not remove much bacteria. Furthermore, because the washing process inevitably causes water to splash around the sink, the act of washing actually spreads the bacteria found in some chicken. If your chicken is dripping after removing it from the package, just blot it with paper towels and quickly dispose of them. —**John Mulvaney**, corporate culinary trainer

Soto Ayam
(Indonesian Chicken and Vegetable Soup)

This chicken soup is cherished all across Indonesia, where our service staff hail from and are trained. Recipes vary widely, but the palate-cleansing effects of its tart spiciness make it the perfect starter for many meals.

FOR THE FRIED ONIONS

Cut onions in half lengthwise. Cut each half crosswise into even slices about ⅛-inch thick, then cut slices into halves or thirds to make smaller arcs. Into a cast-iron skillet or other heavy pan, pour canola or peanut oil to a depth of 1 inch and heat to 300°F. Add about a third of the onions and cook, stirring often, until lightly browned (4 to 5 minutes). Oil temperature will drop at first, but rise again as the onions brown; regulate heat to maintain 300°F. With a slotted spoon, remove onions and drain on a plate lined with paper towels. Repeat with remaining onions; reserve.

FOR THE SOUP

Heat oil in a wok or large saucepan over medium heat. Add chicken, garlic, ginger, and shrimp paste and cook, stirring, for 2 minutes without browning. Add chicken broth, turmeric, and coconut milk; bring to a boil. Add *daun salam* or curry leaves. Reduce heat and simmer, uncovered, for 15 to 20 minutes.

Just before serving, add reserved fried onions, celery, and noodles; let boil for 1 minute. Stir in scallions and lemon juice and season with salt and pepper. Ladle soup into warm soup bowls and garnish with lemon and egg wedges and chopped tomato. Offer chili sauce as a condiment.

NOTES

- *Daun salam* are Indonesian bay leaves. If they are unavailable, do not substitute bay leaves, whose flavor they don't resemble, but seek out curry leaves, which are somewhat similar in flavor and are available from Indian grocery stores.

- Asian chili sauce is available at Indian and Southeast Asian markets and in the ethnic foods section of many supermarkets.

YIELD: 8 SERVINGS

FRIED ONIONS

2 medium onions

1–2 cups canola or peanut oil, for frying

SOUP

1 tablespoon peanut or canola oil

1 pound chicken breast, poached and shredded

1 clove garlic, crushed

1 teaspoon grated ginger

1 teaspoon shrimp paste (available from Asian grocery stores)

5 cups chicken broth (see Pantry Staples)

1 teaspoon ground turmeric

½ cup coconut milk

2 *daun salam* or curry leaves (see Notes)

1 cup thinly sliced celery

3–5 ounces dried bean thread noodles (also known as cellophane noodles), soaked in cold water for 15 minutes and then drained

½ cup sliced scallions (white and light green parts only)

1 tablespoon fresh lemon juice

Salt

Freshly ground black pepper

1 lemon, cut into 8 wedges, for garnish

4 hard-boiled eggs, quartered, for garnish

2 medium tomatoes, seeded and chopped, for garnish

Asian chili sauce (*sambal*), to taste (see Notes)

CHAPTER 9

BEEF, LAMB, VEAL, & VENISON

Just as every ship has a captain, the leader who ensures a smooth sailing experience, every restaurant or hotel kitchen has an executive chef. This chef is responsible for creating fine dining experiences for guests. But when the main course is meat, the most important person involved is the butcher. Each Holland America Line ship has its own butcher—the chief *boucher*. The head butcher is the captain of every plate of *carne* served. Deep in the ship are unique storerooms of treasure—one filled with beef delivered fresh every week, and aged for use on board ship; another frosty "walk in" storeroom for lamb; and yet another for poultry, and so on. The butcher is responsible for everything that goes in and out of these

The mermaid art (left) was the cover of the farewell dinner menu on the *Nieuw Amsterdam* on Tuesday, January 2, 1968; the artwork for the map of America was also used in 1968 on a dinner menu for Tuesday, October 15.

storerooms, and the value of the cache—both culinary- and money-wise—is tremendous.

All of the cutting of the meat is done on the ship in designated cutting rooms by a team of butchers—about forty-five hundred portions of meat a day are prepared. Using the daily menu as their guide, the butchers cut and portion the desired pieces. Our butchers also make all of the marinades and marinate the meats according to the menu plans. They count, cut, and bag meat into individual portions for each cooking

A TASTE OF EXCELLENCE

CLASSIC MARGARITA

Rolando Navoa, bartender

There are as many different stories about how the margarita originated as there are versions of this popular drink. Tequila, however, is the key ingredient.

2 wedges lime

1½ ounces tequila

1½ ounces triple sec

2 ounces homemade sour mix (see Pantry Staples)

1 ounce soda water

Coarse salt, for rim

In a pint glass, hand-press lime wedges with a muddler. Fill glass with ice. Add tequila, triple sec, sour mix, and soda water. Cap with shaker can and shake vigorously. Pour into a pint glass with a salted rim. Serve with a straw.   YIELD: 1 DRINK

station—sautéing, roasting, grilling, braising—in the galley above. The bones and scraps get delivered to the sauciers for sauces and stocks. It's an amazing orchestration of logistics, quality control, art, and care.

With a little planning and the right ingredients, you can create any of these hearty dishes at home. To make these recipes at home and have them turn out as beautifully as you remember from your trip, you won't need an army of cooks, or even a live-in *boucher*; all you need is the recipes on these pages, and high-quality fresh meats.

Of special note in this chapter is the Beef *Kari-Kari*, which is oxtail in peanut sauce. This recipe originated as "crew food"—the menu of meals served to our dedicated staff. This dish is so delicious that it has been brought up to our Lido restaurants. It's one of the specialties of our Filipino chefs, and it may just become a new favorite chez vous.

CHEF'S NOTE FROM THE GALLEY

MARTIN GROENENDYK
Executive chef

For a faster-cooking burger, push your finger in the center of the patties about half the depth of the burger to form an indention. This little trick allows the heat to circulate more evenly and the hamburger to cook faster. Always remember to wash your hands after handling uncooked meats.

Grilled Filet Mignon Pepper Steaks with Green Peppercorn Sauce

4 (6- to 8-ounce) filet mignon steaks (each about 1-inch thick)

4 tablespoons dried green peppercorns (see Notes)

2 tablespoons black peppercorns

2 tablespoons Dijon mustard

1 tablespoon unsalted butter

1 onion, finely chopped

3 tablespoons cognac or brandy

½ cup beef or veal demi-glace (see Notes)

½ cup whipping cream

Salt

Creamed Spinach, optional (see Side Dishes)

Potatoes Gratinée, optional (see Side Dishes)

Mushroom Brochette, optional (see Side Dishes)

Sautéed Asparagus, optional

Finely chopped chives, for garnish

Pepper is used worldwide to bring hot taste and pungent aroma to dishes both savory and sweet. It is an appetite stimulant as well as a digestive, which can only mean it was put on this earth for us to enjoy. We hope you do!

Wipe steaks with a damp cloth. In a mortar and pestle, coarsely crush 2 tablespoons dried green peppercorns and all the black peppercorns, or place them in a cloth and crush with a rolling pin. Rub 1 side of each steak with mustard. Press mustard-side of steaks firmly into peppercorn mixture. Cover steaks with plastic wrap and let marinate for 30 minutes.

Meanwhile, soak the remaining 2 tablespoons green peppercorns in warm water until plump; drain and set aside.

Melt butter in skillet over medium-high heat. Add onion and soaked green peppercorns and sauté for 2 minutes. Add cognac and cook, stirring, until almost evaporated. Add demi-glace and cream and simmer until mixture thickens to sauce consistency and coats the back of a spoon, about 6 minutes. Season sauce with salt; reserve (keep warm). (Sauce can be prepared 1 day ahead. Cover and refrigerate. Bring to a simmer before using.)

Prepare grill (medium-high heat) or preheat broiler. Season steaks generously with salt. Starting peppercorn-side down, grill or broil steaks to desired doneness, about 3 to 4 minutes per side for medium-rare. Transfer steaks to plates. Spoon green peppercorn sauce around steaks. Serve with creamed spinach and potatoes gratinée, if desired.

NOTES

- Dried green peppercorns are available at specialty food shops or from mail order spice houses. If you cannot find them, rub steaks with crushed black peppercorns only. For the sauce, you may use canned green peppercorns packed in brine; drain before using and store any unused portion for up to a month, well covered, in the refrigerator.

- Demi-glace, a mainstay in any professional French kitchen, is a thick glaze made from reducing brown sauce with beef stock or veal stock and Madeira or sherry. It can take a home cook up to 2 days to make a demi-glace from scratch. To save time, you can order demi-glace online from several manufacturers or buy demi-glace in jars from specialty food shops. Because the strength of purchased demi-glace can vary, follow manufacturer's instructions when using it.

Grilled Lamb Chops with Oregano and Apple Chutney

In this easy-to-make-ahead recipe, tender marinated lamb chops are accompanied by a flavor-packed spicy apple chutney.

FOR THE APPLE CHUTNEY

In a small nonreactive saucepan, combine ⅓ cup sugar, water, ground ginger, chili sauce, jalapeño, and lime juice. Bring to a boil, stirring to dissolve the sugar. Boil for 2 minutes. Remove from heat and let cool; strain into a bowl and set aside.

In a medium skillet, melt butter over medium-high heat. Add apples, onion, and fresh ginger and sauté for 5 minutes, until apple and onion are tender. In a small bowl whisk remaining ¼ cup sugar, cider vinegar, and apple juice; add to apples along with currants. Cook, stirring, for 1 minute.

Add lemon zest and reserved chili syrup to apples. Bring to a boil, stirring, for 2 minutes, until mixture is loose and chutneylike. Remove from heat and let cool to room temperature. Fold in mint. Cover and refrigerate until ready to use.

FOR THE LAMB CHOPS

In a glass dish, stir together honey, red wine vinegar, garlic, oregano, salt, and pepper. Add lamb, turning to coat. Marinate lamb, chilled, turning often, for 1 hour. Bring lamb to room temperature before grilling.

Prepare grill. When fire is medium-hot (you can hold your hand 5 inches above rack for 3 to 4 seconds), grill lamb on lightly oiled grill rack, turning once, about 4 minutes total for medium-rare. (The chops should register 120° to 135°F at the thickest part for rare to medium rare.)

Alternately, lamb can be grilled in batches in a lightly oiled well-seasoned ridged grill pan over medium-high heat. Or you can broil them 3 inches from the flame for 3 minutes per side.

Transfer lamb to plates and spoon apple chutney alongside. Garnish with oregano sprigs and serve immediately.

NOTE

To french bones, scrape or cut an inch or two of meat from the ends of the bones. You can ask your butcher to do this for you.

YIELD: 4 SERVINGS

APPLE CHUTNEY

⅓ cup plus ¼ cup sugar

⅓ cup water

¼ teaspoon ground ginger

¼ teaspoon hot chili sauce, such as sriacha

¼ teaspoon finely minced fresh jalapeño

Juice from ¼ lime

2 tablespoons salted butter

2 medium green apples, peeled, cored, and cut into ¼-inch chunks

1 medium white onion, cut into ¼-inch chunks

1 teaspoon very finely minced fresh ginger

¼ cup cider vinegar

½ cup apple juice

1½ tablespoons dried currants

½ teaspoon finely grated lemon zest

2 tablespoons minced fresh mint

LAMB CHOPS

2 tablespoons honey

2 tablespoons red wine vinegar

2 cloves garlic, finely chopped

2 teaspoons finely chopped fresh oregano leaves, preferably Greek oregano

½ teaspoon salt

¼ teaspoon freshly ground black pepper

8 rib lamb chops (1½ pounds total), bones frenched and all fat trimmed (see Note)

8 sprigs thyme, for garnish

Thyme Roasted Venison Fillet with
Red Onion-Raisin Compote and Poached Figs

YIELD: 6 SERVINGS

RED ONION-RAISIN COMPOTE

2 quarts venison stock
(see Pantry Staples)

4 tablespoons sugar

¼ cup red wine vinegar

½ cup unsalted butter

5 large red onions, cut into eighths

¾ cup raisins

1 tablespoon cornstarch

Salt

Freshly ground white pepper

POACHED FIGS

¾ cup red wine

2 tablespoons sugar

12 firm-ripe fresh purple figs

THYME-ROASTED VENISON

6 (6-ounce) venison fillets

Salt

Freshly ground black pepper

2 tablespoons fresh thyme leaves,
chopped

2 tablespoons canola oil

TO ASSEMBLE

Vegetable cooking spray

Creamy Polenta (see Side Dishes)

12 sprigs thyme, for garnish

F arm-raised venison is very mild and readily available, so try it if you haven't! Just be sure to serve venison rare to medium, as it is a very lean meat that toughens and develops a strong flavor if overcooked.

FOR THE RED ONION-RAISIN COMPOTE

Bring venison stock to a simmer and reduce by half to 1 quart. Meanwhile, in a medium nonreactive saucepan, heat sugar, stirring constantly, over medium-high heat. When golden brown, add vinegar and butter. Bring to a boil. When sugar has dissolved, add onions, raisins, and reduced stock. Bring to a boil, reduce heat to medium, and simmer for 45 minutes.

In a small bowl, combine cornstarch and 1 tablespoon water to make a sauce consistency. Whisk this cornstarch mixture into onion mixture and stir until thickened. Season with salt and pepper. (Add more sugar and/or vinegar to achieve a sweet-and-sour balance.) Remove from heat and set aside.

FOR THE POACHED FIGS

Simmer wine with sugar in a nonreactive saucepan that is just large enough to hold figs upright, stirring until sugar is dissolved. Cut a very thin slice from the bottom of each fig and stand figs in liquid in saucepan (figs will not be covered by liquid). Poach figs at a bare simmer, covered, for 5 minutes. Cool slightly in liquid.

FOR THE THYME-ROASTED VENISON

Preheat oven to 425°F. Season fillets with salt and pepper and rub thyme into them. In a large ovenproof heavy pan or cast-iron skillet, heat oil over high heat until quite hot. Add fillets to pan and sear until browned on one side, about 2 minutes. Turn venison over and place pan in oven for 6 minutes, or until venison is slightly pink in the middle and an instant read thermometer inserted in the center registers 135°F. Remove, transfer to a platter, and let rest for 10 minutes.

TO ASSEMBLE AND SERVE

Spray grill with cooking spray and light. Cut polenta into 6 squares. Cut each square diagonally into 2 triangles. Spray polenta with oil spray. Grill until heated through over medium heat, about 5 minutes per side. Spoon some compote on warmed plates. Slice venison fillets on the diagonal and fan in the center. Arrange 2 figs and 2 grilled polenta triangles on each plate. Garnish with thyme sprigs and serve immediately.

Rack of Veal with Roasted Vegetables and Thyme Glaze

W hen you want to serve something special—really special—at home, it's got to be rack of veal. It's such a fancy cut, you should order it in advance from a butcher.

FOR THE VEAL

Preheat oven to 500°F. Pat veal dry thoroughly with paper towels (veal is a very moist meat and you want it to brown rather than steam). In a small bowl, combine salt, pepper, 2 tablespoons thyme leaves, parsley, garlic, and olive oil. Rub veal thoroughly with this mixture, pressing herbs to adhere, and place it in a roasting pan. Transfer to oven and roast for about 20 minutes, or until well browned.

Reduce oven temperature to 300°F. Roast veal for 20 to 40 minutes more, inserting an instant-read thermometer in the thickest part of the meat to determine the doneness you prefer (126°F for medium rare, 134°F for medium, or 150°F for medium-well). Remove pan from oven, transfer veal to a warm platter, and allow to rest for 10 minutes, tented with foil.

FOR THE SAUCE

Tilt roasting pan and spoon off and discard any fat, leaving drippings behind. Place pan over medium heat and add wine, stirring to dissolve any solids stuck in the bottom of the pan. Scrape contents of pan into a large glass measuring cup or a medium saucepan; reserve.

Heat butter in skillet over medium heat. Add shallots and cook, stirring, until starting to turn brown. Add 1 cup chopped thyme and cook, stirring, for 30 seconds. Add reserved pan drippings and vinegar; reduce liquid by half. Add veal stock reduction and bay leaf. Simmer until sauce thickens and coats the back of a spoon. Pour any collected juices from veal roast into sauce in skillet; heat through, about 1 minute. Season with salt and pepper and strain into a saucepan; keep warm.

TO SERVE

Cut veal into chops and divide among warmed plates. Spoon sauce over and around chops and serve immediately with roasted vegetables, if desired.

YIELD: 6–7 SERVINGS

1 (7-bone) rack of veal (about 5 pounds), frenched

2 tablespoons sea salt, plus extra to taste

2 tablespoons freshly ground black pepper, plus extra to taste

2 tablespoons fresh thyme leaves, plus 1 cup chopped fresh thyme

¼ cup chopped fresh parsley

2 tablespoons finely minced garlic

¼ cup olive oil

2 cups white wine

2 tablespoons unsalted butter

3 large shallots, chopped (about ⅔ cup)

2 tablespoons sherry vinegar

4 cups veal stock reduced by half with ½ tablespoon tomato paste (see Pantry Staples)

1 bay leaf

Roasted Vegetables, optional (see Side Dishes)

Beef *Kari-Kari*

2 pounds chuck steak or 4 pounds oxtails

2 tablespoons vegetable oil, plus 5 tablespoons more for browning

1 tablespoon annatto seeds or 1 teaspoon paprika plus a pinch of turmeric

2 medium onions, chopped

2 cloves garlic, crushed

1 cup celery root, roughly chopped

2 cups beef broth or stock (see Pantry Staples)

¾ pound new potatoes, peeled and cut into large dice

2 tablespoons tamarind sauce (see Notes)

1 tablespoon fish sauce or anchovy sauce, such as Worcestershire

2 teaspoons sugar

1 bay leaf

1 sprig fresh thyme

3 tablespoons roasted long-grain rice, finely ground (see Notes)

½ cup roasted skinless peanuts, blended, or 3 tablespoons natural peanut butter

1 tablespoon white wine vinegar

Salt

Freshly ground black pepper

6 heads baby bok choy, rinsed and pan steamed in ½ cup salted water until base is tender, for garnish

3 small Japanese eggplants, sliced and sautéed, for garnish

Bagoong (optional; see Notes)

The food from the Philippines is influenced by the Spanish, but *kari-kari* retains much of its Asian origins. Often made with the deep purplish banana flower, it is a favorite dish of our many talented kitchen crew members from that Southeast Asian country.

Cut beef into 1-inch cubes and set aside. (If using oxtails, cut into 3-inch pieces.) Heat 2 tablespoons oil in a large flameproof casserole. Add annatto seeds and stir until oil turns dark red. With a slotted spoon, remove seeds and discard. (If using paprika and turmeric, simply stir into oil.)

Add onion, garlic, and celery root to annatto oil in casserole. Fry until softened, 3 to 5 minutes. With a slotted spoon, transfer vegetables to a bowl; set aside. Add enough of the remaining oil to the casserole to coat it and place over high heat. When oil is hot but not yet smoking, add beef cubes (or oxtail)—in batches, if necessary, to avoid overcrowding—and cook until lightly and evenly browned. Add reserved vegetables, broth, potatoes, tamarind sauce, fish sauce, sugar, bay leaf, and thyme. Bring to a simmer; reduce heat to low, cover, and cook until meat is tender, about 2 hours.

Meanwhile, in a medium bowl combine ground rice and roasted blended peanuts (or peanut butter). Stir about 4 tablespoons beef cooking liquid into nut mixture; transfer the mixture into the casserole, stirring it in.

Simmer the stew gently, uncovered, until thickened, about 15 to 20 minutes. Stir in vinegar and season with salt and pepper. Garnish with steamed baby bok choy, and eggplant; serve with *bagoong*, if desired.

NOTES

- To make tamarind sauce, purchase a small block of cellophane-wrapped tamarind paste from an Asian grocery store. Cut off a chunk of the block and soak it in enough warm water to loosen and remove the seeds. Press through a strainer and discard any seeds, fiber, or skin. Then measure 2 tablespoons from the strained juice and pulp.

- Roast rice in a heavy frying pan without oil and stir constantly to let grains gradually become a deep golden color. Cool and pulverize in a blender or coffee grinder. Sift through a strainer and discard coarse pieces.

- *Bagoong* is a salty condiment (and flavoring) made from shrimp or small fish that have been salted, cured, and fermented for several weeks. It's the traditional accompaniment to *kari-kari*. *Bagoong* is available from Philippine grocery stores or from online sources.

CHAPTER 10

VEGETARIAN FARE

Despite the fact that every cuisine on earth contains some variation of all-vegetarian dishes, to me, it is an important category of cuisine unto itself. | In the same way that someone with a taste for meat or fish will look for the *pesce* or *carne* sections of a menu, someone with a craving for a meatless meal should not have to search through a menu for what they seek. And, naturally, some people eat meatless meals exclusively, so including a vegetarian section on all menus, as we do at Holland America Line, makes a lot of sense. | Vegetarian cuisine, which today is a distinct and distinctive branch of the culinary arts, is about what all other fine food is about—tasting and looking great.

On every Holland America Line ship, there is one specially trained vegetarian chef, whose exclusive responsibility is preparing our extensive all-vegetarian offerings.

Our chefs of vegetarian cuisine have a solid background in the foundations of classic cooking techniques, but then receive further training in the culinary specialization required in cooking with no meat, poultry, or fish stocks whatsoever. These chefs excel at taking eggs, cheese, and grains to form a nutritious base for interesting vegetarian combinations, like our wildly popular Holland America Line signature dish Eggplant Rollatini Gratinée on Mushroom Risotto with Marinara Sauce. As with any fine meal,

Playful illustrations of a ship and an anchor made of food were featured on the covers of *Maasdam* dinner menus from October 1955.

FRESH GRAPEFRUIT "NOT A COSMO"

Arnel Dineros, bartender

When it comes to liquid refreshment, great taste does not always have to mean alcohol.

2 wedges lime

⅛ of a grapefruit

2 ounces homemade sour mix (see Pantry Staples)

1 ounce cranberry juice cocktail

1½ ounces soda water

1 long zest of fresh grapefruit

In a pint glass, hand-press lime wedges and grapefruit with a muddler. Fill glass with ice. Add sour mix, cranberry juice cocktail, and soda water. Cap with shaker can and shake vigorously. Strain into a chilled martini glass and garnish with grapefruit twist across the rim.

YIELD: 1 DRINK

ingredients need to be fresh and of optimal quality, the preparation has to be executed carefully, and of course, there's the whole aspect of culinary creativity and excellence from which vegetarian cookery should not be exempt.

I would recommend that when you try these recipes at home, picture them as you would have encountered them in one of Holland America Line's stellar dining rooms: they should look special and be as beautifully presented as any entrée of meat, poultry, or fish.

Any one of these dishes can be adjusted to make a tasty side dish or a sensational appetizer for entertaining. Finally, if you really want to wow your friends at the next potluck you attend, think about bringing along one of these special Holland America Line signature vegetarian dishes, like the Wild Mushroom, Spinach, and Feta Cheese Strudel with Thai Red Curry Sauce. It's simple yet sophisticated, and you may never bring a three-bean casserole again.

CHEF'S NOTE FROM THE GALLEY

THOMAS SCHUMANN
Corporate culinary trainer

One of the most important aspects of cooking with water in any form is the water itself. Regular tap water can destroy the color and flavor of everything it touches, even for steaming. Distilled water is a far better cooking liquid, as all the minerals have been removed.

Wild Mushroom, Spinach, and Feta Cheese Strudel with Thai Red Curry Sauce

1 stick unsalted butter, melted, plus extra if needed

6 cloves garlic, finely minced

½ pound assorted wild mushrooms (such as oyster, cremini, stemmed shiitake, and portobello), sliced

Salt

Freshly ground black pepper

½ pound spinach, tough stems removed, washed well

1 can (14 ounces) coconut milk

½ cup heavy cream

2 teaspoons Thai red curry paste (see Note)

¾ cup apple juice

6 sheets phyllo dough (18 inches x 14 inches), thawed for 24 hours in refrigerator

6 ounces feta cheese, crumbled

½ cup cooked brown lentils (from ¼ cup uncooked)

NOTE

Thai red curry paste is available at Indian and Southeast Asian markets and in the ethnic foods section of many supermarkets.

Texture and flavor abound in this crispy roll, encasing an earthy blend of mushrooms and spinach, perked up with salty feta, and served with a spicy creamy sauce. It makes a terrific appetizer or a perfect light lunch.

FOR THE FILLING

In a skillet, heat 1 tablespoon butter over medium heat. Add garlic and mushrooms and sauté, stirring, until the liquid released by the mushrooms is evaporated. Season with salt and pepper. Transfer to a bowl and let cool.

Heat ½ tablespoon butter in the same skillet over medium heat. Add spinach, cover, and let steam with just the water clinging to the leaves, stirring once, for 3 minutes. Transfer wilted spinach to a colander and push out excess liquid. On a cutting board, chop spinach coarsely; place in a bowl and season with salt and pepper.

FOR THE SAUCE

In a small saucepan, bring coconut milk, cream, and curry paste to a simmer over medium-low heat. Cook, stirring, for 20 to 30 minutes, until flavors blend. Season with salt and pepper. Add enough apple juice to reach a sauce consistency; reserve (keep warm).

FOR THE STRUDEL

Preheat oven to 400°F. Lightly coat a baking sheet with butter or nonstick cooking spray.

Lay 1 sheet of phyllo on a work surface. (Keep the remaining phyllo covered with a damp kitchen towel and plastic wrap.) With a pastry brush, brush the phyllo sheet lightly with some melted butter. Top with a second sheet of phyllo. Repeat with the remaining phyllo sheets, brushing with butter between each layer, until you have a stack.

Spread mushrooms, spinach, crumbled feta cheese, and lentils on dough. Starting on 1 long edge, roll up the phyllo into a cylinder, folding the short edges in to make a tight seal.

Place the strudel seam-side down on the prepared baking sheet. Brush with melted butter. Bake for 25 minutes, or until golden brown and crisp. Slice and serve immediately with the red curry sauce.

Eggplant Rollatini Gratinée
on Mushroom Risotto with Marinara Sauce

EGGPLANT

2 medium eggplants, sliced into 16 lengthwise slices ¼- to ⅓-inch thick

Sea salt

Vegetable cooking spray

MARINARA SAUCE

½ cup virgin olive oil

1 onion, finely chopped

2 teaspoons finely chopped garlic

1 pound fresh tomatoes, peeled, seeded, and chopped (see Tip, page 86) or 1 (15-ounce) can whole tomatoes, seeded and chopped briefly in a food processor

½ cup tomato paste

2 teaspoons dried basil, crushed

2 teaspoons dried oregano, crushed

1 bay leaf

Salt

Freshly ground black pepper

Sugar, if needed

ROLLATINI FILLING

12 ounces ricotta cheese

12 ounces cream cheese

1 teaspoon finely chopped garlic

1 teaspoon chopped fresh oregano

1 teaspoon chopped fresh basil

2 egg yolks

Salt

Freshly ground black pepper

TO ASSEMBLE

Olive oil, for greasing

1 pound mozzarella cheese, grated

½ cup grated Parmesan cheese

Mushroom Risotto, optional (see Pasta and Risotto)

It's a delightful surprise to discover something hidden inside a roll (or wrapper). These savory cylinders sit atop risotto and are smothered in marinara and topped with browned cheese—which can make getting to the filling quite a delicious adventure.

FOR THE EGGPLANT

Arrange eggplant slices on a rack over a large baking sheet. Sprinkle with sea salt and set aside for 1 hour or more to help remove any bitter juices. Rinse off salt very well and pat eggplant dry with a towel. Spray a hot ridged grill pan liberally with vegetable spray (or use a double-sided electric grill) and add eggplant slices in batches without crowding. Grill until lightly browned and tender, about 3 minutes per side. Remove slices from the grill pan and allow to cool; reserve.

FOR THE MARINARA SAUCE

Heat oil in a heavy large skillet over medium heat. Add onion and sauté until translucent, about 10 minutes. Add garlic and sauté for 1 minute. Add tomatoes and their juices. Cover and simmer for 15 minutes. Add tomato paste and herbs. Season with salt and pepper. Cover and cook for 15 minutes, stirring occasionally. Uncover and cook for 5 more minutes. Add a bit of sugar if necessary, to counter any acidity or sharpness; reserve.

FOR THE ROLLATINI FILLING

In a medium bowl, whisk all the ingredients together. Cover and refrigerate until needed.

TO ASSEMBLE

Preheat oven to 350°F. Grease a 13-inch x 9-inch x 2-inch glass baking dish with olive oil. Spread cannelloni filling evenly on eggplant slices. Starting at 1 short end, roll up eggplant slices, enclosing filling. Arrange rolls, seam side down, in prepared baking dish. Top evenly with marinara sauce and bake for about 10 minutes. Evenly sprinkle mozzarella and Parmesan cheese on top and brown under the broiler. To serve, divide mushroom risotto (if using) among plates. Place 2 eggplant rolls with their toppings on each risotto mound and serve immediately.

Asparagus and Sautéed Mushrooms with Black Pepper Romano Cheese Zabaglione

This savory zabaglione is so much lighter than a hollandaise, and its foamy essence tickles the tongue with flavor. Though this dish makes a wonderful meatless appetizer, there's no better sidekick to a grilled steak.

Bring a large saucepan of salted water to a boil. With a vegetable peeler, pare down the base of large asparagus spears to remove any fibrous outer layer; reserve.

While salted water heats, bring about 1 inch of water to a simmer in a wide saucepan. Adjust the heat so that the water is at a bare simmer. In a large heatproof mixing bowl that can sit on the saucepan, combine egg yolks, 2 teaspoons black pepper, white wine, and Marsala. With an electric mixer, beat yolks until pale in color, stopping 2 or 3 times to scrape down the sides of the bowl.

Set the bowl over the pan and whisk constantly until the mixture thickens and is lemony looking, about 8 minutes. Fold 2 tablespoons Pecorino Romano and 1 teaspoon pepper into zabaglione. Reserve (keep warm).

In a large skillet, heat butter over medium-high heat. When the foam subsides, add mushrooms and sauté, stirring, until tender. Season with salt and pepper and reserve (keep warm).

TO SERVE

Place reserved asparagus in the boiling salted water and cook until just tender but still bright green, 3 to 5 minutes. Drain immediately, dry on paper towels, and divide between 2 plates. Add mushrooms to asparagus and top vegetables with some zabaglione. Sprinkle with the remaining 1 tablespoon cheese and drizzle with a little lemon juice and olive oil.

YIELD: 2 SERVINGS

Salt

12 medium or jumbo asparagus

4 egg yolks

3 teaspoons freshly ground black pepper

²⁄₃ cup white wine

Dash of Marsala

3 tablespoons grated Pecorino Romano cheese

2 tablespoons unsalted butter

½ pound fresh shiitake mushrooms, stems discarded and caps sliced

Fresh lemon juice, for drizzling

Olive oil, for drizzling

TIP | If you like the taste of chiles in your food but want to cut down on the "heat," remove some of the white veinlike material (the ribs) that holds the seeds in the pepper. The spicy chemical capsaicin is produced in the ribs, which makes the ribs—not the seeds—the hottest part of the chile. —**Ed Sayomac**, executive chef

Indian Vegetable Curry

3 tablespoons vegetable oil

1 medium onion, peeled and chopped

2 medium carrots, peeled and chopped

8 ounces mushrooms, halved

1 red bell pepper, cored, seeded, and cut into strips

2 cloves garlic, crushed

½ tablespoon grated fresh ginger

1 teaspoon ground cumin

½ tablespoon curry powder

1 teaspoon ground turmeric

2 medium tomatoes, peeled, seeded, and chopped (see Tip, page 86)

½ cup unsalted sliced almonds

2–3 cups vegetable stock, canned or homemade, as needed (see Pantry Staples)

8 thin-to-medium spears asparagus, trimmed and cut into 2-inch lengths

1 cup green beans, trimmed and cut into 1-inch lengths

½ cup sugar snap peas, trimmed

1 (8-ounce) can baby corn, rinsed and drained

2 apples, peeled, cored, and chopped

Salt

Freshly ground black pepper

¼ cup coconut cream (see Note)

6 cups cooked basmati rice

1 bunch fresh cilantro, chopped

¼ cup mango chutney

4 small wedges fresh pineapple, for garnish

Vegetable curries take less time to cook than meat curries, so they are a tasty and healthful weeknight dinner option. They're also a great way to combine the vegetables you love best, so experiment! If you want to serve wine with a curry, a semi-dry Riesling can be a good complement. Otherwise, serve beer or cups of fragrant tea.

In a soup pot, heat oil over medium heat. Add onion, carrots, mushrooms, and bell pepper. Cook, stirring, until onions are golden brown, about 15 minutes. Add garlic, ginger, cumin, curry powder, and turmeric. Cook, stirring, for 5 minutes more. Stir in tomatoes. Reduce heat to low, cover, and cook for 10 minutes more.

Meanwhile, in a dry skillet over high heat, stir almonds, taking care not to scorch them, until lightly browned. Transfer them to a small bowl and let cool.

Add enough vegetable stock to just cover vegetables and bring to a boil. Reduce heat and simmer, stirring occasionally, for 10 minutes. Add asparagus, green beans, snap peas, baby corn, and apples; cook for 5 minutes more. Season with salt and pepper.

Grind half the almonds in a spice grinder and transfer to a small bowl. Add coconut cream and stir to make a paste. Carefully stir coconut paste into the simmering vegetables and heat through.

To serve, mound basmati rice in the center of warmed plates and spoon vegetable curry around mounds. Sprinkle curry with the remaining sliced almonds and chopped cilantro. Place a dollop of chutney on each plate. Top rice with pineapple wedge and serve immediately.

NOTE

Coconut cream is available from Indian grocery stores. Do not use sweetened cream of coconut. If you cannot find coconut cream, you can use the cream from the top of canned coconut milk (you'll need 2 cans coconut milk to get ¼ cup coconut cream).

Sautéed Vegetable "Spaghetti" with Portobello Mushroom, Tomato Coulis, and Pesto Sauce

There's no pasta on this plate, just thin strands of vegetables cooked al dente and topped with two sauces. This makes a colorful, light main course or an unusual and toothsome side dish.

FOR THE TOMATO COULIS

Heat 2 tablespoons olive oil in a large saucepan over medium heat. Add garlic and cook, stirring, for 30 seconds. Add tomatoes and reduce heat to low; cook, stirring occasionally, for about 45 minutes. Season with salt, pepper, and sugar. Continue cooking for about 1 hour, skimming off any clear liquid. Stir in minced basil. (Coulis may be kept, covered, in the refrigerator for up to 5 days.)

FOR THE "SPAGHETTI"

Bring a large pot of salted water to a boil. Prepare a large bowl of ice water. Add carrot strands to boiling water and blanch for 30 seconds. With a strainer, remove carrots and plunge them into the ice water to stop the cooking. Remove from ice water and drain on a plate lined with paper towels. Repeat procedure with zucchini and yellow squash.

TO SERVE

In a large skillet, heat 1 tablespoon oil over medium heat. Add portobello mushroom caps, top-side down, and sauté until nicely golden, about 1 to 2 minutes. Flip and cook, covered, until slightly softened, about 1 minute more. Transfer to individual plates. Wipe skillet. Heat 1 remaining tablespoon oil in skillet over medium heat. Add reserved carrot, zucchini, and squash "spaghetti" and cook, gently stirring, until just heated through. Remove from heat and add pesto sauce; toss gently to coat. Place "spaghetti" on mushrooms and top with some tomato coulis. Serve immediately.

> TIP Tofu makes a terrific addition to stir-fries, stews, and even salads. But for maximum flavor and texture, you need to press out the liquid and sauté the tofu. To do this, take a block of firm or extra firm tofu and wrap it in 1 or 2 kitchen towels. Place on a plate, top with a cutting board, and weigh down the board with a large can of vegetables. After 20 minutes or so, remove tofu from towels and cut into ½-inch cubes. Season cubes with salt and brown them in oil in a hot skillet without crowding or turning too often, so that they get a golden brown crust on one or more sides. —**Thomas Krieger,** executive chef

YIELD: 2 SERVINGS

4 tablespoons olive oil

1 clove garlic, finely minced

5 pounds tomatoes, peeled, seeded, and chopped (see Tip, page 86)

Salt

Freshly ground black pepper

½ tablespoon sugar

1 tablespoon minced basil, plus 2 whole leaves basil for garnish

2 carrots, cut into strands with a spiral slicer (see Note)

2 zucchini, cut into strands with a spiral slicer

2 yellow summer squash, cut into strands with a spiral slicer

2 large portobello mushrooms, stemmed

½ cup pesto sauce, store-bought or homemade (see Pantry Staples)

NOTE

Spiral slicers turn almost any firm vegetable into fine spaghetti-like strands or incredibly thin long ribbons. (Look for the Benriner brand.) In addition to vegetable spaghetti, you can use them to make fried carrot garnishes, potato nests, or elegant fruit or vegetable salads. If you don't own a spiral slicer, cut matchstick strips or slices with a mandoline.

CHAPTER 11

SIDE DISHES

At Holland America Line we stay ahead of the culinary trends, but we also hold on to the classics, because what makes a dish classic are the same things that make anything classic: integrity, refinement, and near-universal popularity. | If you look at the recipes in this chapter, you will see old favorites. It was very much by design that we selected traditional sides such as sautéed carrots, creamed spinach, and various versions of mashed potatoes. Side dishes are the "accessories" to the meal. A side dish rounds out the plate and provides an opportunity to create a unique presentation—perhaps even a tiny bit of showmanship. Elegance and excellence, both in visuals and taste, rely on a balance of color, texture, and proportion.

This platter of sides includes (from top to bottom) the Creamed Spinach with Parmesan Wafer, Baby Carrots and Asparagus, Potatoes Gratinée, and a Mushroom Brochette.

On Holland America Line, you are served your main course in one presentation, so the chef has control over how your plate will look when it arrives at your place setting.

We take great care to "turn" even a carrot. Far below the galley decks, where the provisions are stored, vegetable cooks, also known as *commis cook entremetier*, spend the day preparing the vegetables for side dishes.

PRICKLY PINEAPPLE DAIQUIRI

Jerry Sabino, bartender

Holland America Line offers a tantalizing selection of daiquiris carefully crafted with Captain Morgan's Spiced Rum and fresh citrus juices. Here's one with the vivid color of prickly pear.

2 wedges lime

1½ ounces spiced rum

2 ounces homemade sour mix (see Pantry Staples)

1 ounce pineapple juice

1 ounce soda water

Prickly pear purée, for drizzling (see Note)

In a pint glass, hand-press lime wedges with a muddler. Fill glass with ice. Add rum, sour mix, pineapple juice, and soda water. Cap with shaker can and shake vigorously. Pour into a pint glass and drizzle with some prickly pear purée. Serve with a straw.

YIELD: 1 DRINK

NOTE: Prickly pears are the fruit that grow on top of the flat cactus pad; when peeled, the pulp has a delicate melon-fig taste. To make prickly pear purée, wash and peel ripe prickly pears. Halve and scoop out seeds. Force the raw pulp through a medium to fine strainer and freeze it in a sealed freezer container. Thaw before using. Alternatively, you can buy 30-ounce frozen containers of The Perfect Puree's prickly pear purée from online sources.

TONY TUDLA
Executive chef

Always season vegetables when they are almost finished cooking in order to keep their firmness. If you season them too early they will not have as much flavor and can even become wilted. In most cases, adding a little bit of sugar will bring out the flavor, especially with carrots, peas, broccoli, Brussels sprouts, and cauliflower.

A side dish served with meat or fish can make or break the best of meals. At Holland America Line, each side dish is as delicious, beautiful, and fully considered as any main dish. The recipes in this chapter are classic, easy to make, and can be used to complement just about any main course you dream up. I would suggest that rather than serve your side dishes in a bowl for self-service, take control of your presentation, and see what happens when you plate all of the elements of your meal yourself. I guarantee you will enjoy this artistic process, and those that you are serving will appreciate your efforts.

Vegetable Risotto

YIELD: 4–6 MAIN-COURSE
SERVINGS, 6–8 SIDE-DISH
SERVINGS

¼ cup diced green zucchini
(¼-inch dice)

¼ cup diced yellow summer squash
(¼-inch dice)

¼ cup diced asparagus (½-inch dice)

¼ cup diced carrots (¼-inch dice)

¼ cup diced red bell peppers
(¼-inch dice)

¼ cup diced green bell peppers
(¼-inch dice)

3 tablespoons unsalted butter

1 small onion, finely chopped

¼ pound fresh button mushrooms,
cleaned, trimmed, and cut into
½-inch dice

6 cups chicken stock, canned or
homemade (see Pantry Staples)

1 pound (2⅓ cups) arborio, carnaroli,
or vialone nano rice

½ cup white wine

½ cup very finely grated Parmesan
cheese

Salt

Freshly ground black pepper

The bright colors and flavors of the vegetables in this risotto come from blanching them beforehand and stirring them in minutes before serving. Enjoy as a side dish or on its own with a crisp salad.

Bring a saucepan of salted water to a boil. Prepare a bowl of ice water. Add zucchini and squash to saucepan and boil until partially cooked, about 2 minutes. With a strainer, remove zucchini and squash and plunge them into ice water to stop the cooking. Drain vegetables, blot dry with paper towels, and place them in a bowl.

Repeat procedure with asparagus (cook for about 2 minutes), carrots (cook for about 3 minutes), and bell peppers (cook for about 2 minutes), boiling each separately until partially cooked, plunging them in ice water, and blotting them dry. Add asparagus, carrots, and bell peppers to zucchini and squash in bowl; set aside.

In a heavy casserole with a thick bottom or enameled cast-iron pot, heat 1 tablespoon butter over medium-high heat. Add onion and cook, stirring, until softened, about 1 minute. Add 1 tablespoon butter and mushrooms to casserole; continue sautéing until any liquid mushrooms give off has evaporated, about 8 minutes.

Meanwhile, bring stock and 2 cups water to a simmer. Keep at a bare simmer, covered.

Add rice to onions and mushrooms, stirring with a wooden spoon so rice is coated with butter, about 1 minute. Add wine and simmer, stirring constantly, until it is absorbed. Stir in ½ cup simmering stock mixture and cook at a strong simmer, stirring frequently, until stock is absorbed. Continue simmering and adding stock ½ cup at a time, stirring frequently and letting each addition become absorbed before adding the next, until rice is tender but still has a slight firmness at the center (the dish should have a creamy texture, like thick soup), about 18 minutes. (There may be leftover stock.)

Stir in reserved blanched vegetables and heat through. If necessary, thin risotto with a little more stock, stirring so rice absorbs all the liquid. Stir in Parmesan and the remaining 1 tablespoon butter. Season with salt and pepper. Serve immediately on warmed dinner plates or shallow soup plates.

Roasted Vegetables

N othing sweetens and concentrates the flavor of vegetables like roasting, and it's very easy to do. Roasted vegetables are a colorful, flavorful partner to countless meat, poultry, or fish preparations. Feel free to substitute your favorite veggies.

Preheat oven to 400°F. In a large bowl, toss onion wedges, garlic cloves, and carrots with enough olive oil to coat lightly. Season with sea salt and pepper and transfer to a roasting pan. Roast for 15 minutes.

Meanwhile, cut steamed potatoes in half and place them in the large bowl. Add mushrooms, zucchini, squash, cherry tomatoes, and rosemary. Toss with enough olive oil to lightly coat and season with salt and pepper.

After the 15 minutes, add remaining vegetables to roasting pan and toss lightly. Continue to roast for 15 more minutes, or until all vegetables are tender.

NOTE

Vegetables can roast while meat roasts, in the same pan or in a different pan on a separate rack. Just add the vegetables to the oven during the last 20 minutes of the meat's roasting time. They can continue to roast while the meat rests, too.

YIELD: 8 SERVINGS

2 medium onions, peeled and quartered lengthwise, with root end left intact

12 cloves garlic, peeled

2 medium carrots, peeled and sliced ½-inch thick

Olive oil

Sea salt and freshly ground black pepper

4 medium red-skinned potatoes, unpeeled and steamed until barely done

1 pound mushrooms, washed and trimmed, large ones halved

1 medium zucchini, sliced ¼-inch thick

1 medium yellow summer squash, sliced ¼-inch thick

16 cherry tomatoes

1 tablespoon chopped fresh rosemary

TIP | When you soak your pots, pans, and grills to make them easier to clean, use the dishwashing detergent that you put in your dishwasher rather than using regular dishwashing soap. After about an hour, the baked or burned on bits will float right off the pan's surface. —**Markus Jenni**, executive chef

Stuffed Eggplants

YIELD: 6 SERVINGS

3 medium eggplants

Salt

½ cup olive oil

1 cup diced onion

3 cloves garlic, crushed

2 ripe medium tomatoes, peeled, seeded, and chopped (see Tip, page 86)

Freshly ground black pepper

1 teaspoon chopped fresh thyme leaves

1 teaspoon ground coriander

1 teaspoon ground cardamom

2 bay leaves

⅓ cup chopped fresh parsley

Fill these eggplants ahead of time and bake them 30 minutes before dinner is served. Their boat shape and warm spicing can provide a rustic Mediterranean complement to lamb or chicken dishes.

Cut eggplants in half lengthwise and scoop the flesh in 1 piece from the center, leaving skin with ⅓ inch of flesh remaining. Sprinkle the inside of each eggplant shell with salt and place cut side down on paper towels.

Dice scooped eggplant and transfer to a colander; sprinkle with salt and let drain for 30 minutes; the salt will help eliminate bitter juices. Rinse with cold water, transfer to a kitchen towel, and twist to remove excess moisture.

Preheat the oven to 300°F. In a deep skillet, heat the oil over medium heat. Add onion and garlic and cook, stirring, until vegetables are translucent. Add diced eggplant and cook until softened. Add tomatoes and remaining ingredients. Increase heat to high and cook, stirring, for 2 to 3 minutes. Season with salt and pepper.

With a paper towel, blot dry interiors of the eggplant shells and fill with tomato mixture. Place in an ovenproof dish and bake for 30 minutes. Serve warm.

Diced Potatoes and Onions

YIELD: 4 SERVINGS

1 pound large red potatoes, peeled, rinsed, and dried

4 tablespoons extra virgin olive oil, plus extra if necessary

½ cup diced onion

1 cup diced smoked ham

1 tablespoon chopped garlic

¼ teaspoon salt

¼ teaspoon freshly ground black pepper

2 tablespoons chopped fresh parsley

Eggs, cooked however you like them, take on a new luster when they sit beside these potatoes. Try them for brunch or dinner.

Dice potatoes into ½-inch cubes. In a heavy skillet, heat oil over medium-high heat. Add onion and cook, stirring, until softened and translucent.

Add potatoes and ham. Cook, stirring, until potatoes are tender in the center (if necessary, add more oil to prevent sticking). Add garlic and cook, stirring, for 2 to 3 minutes more. Do not let garlic brown.

Season vegetables with salt and pepper and transfer to a warmed serving bowl. Sprinkle with parsley and serve immediately.

Creamed Spinach with a Crisp Parmesan Wafer

Always easy, always elegant, creamed spinach ascends to even loftier heights when garnished with a thin Parmesan crisp.

FOR THE CREAMED SPINACH

Place spinach in an 8-quart stockpot, cover, and place over medium heat. Let it steam with just the water clinging to the leaves, stirring once, for 3 minutes. Transfer wilted spinach to a colander and push out excess liquid. On a cutting board, chop spinach coarsely (or, for a smoother texture, chop finely in a food processor); set aside.

In a skillet, heat butter over medium heat. Add garlic; cook, stirring, for 1 minute (do not allow garlic to turn brown). Add flour, salt, and nutmeg; cook, stirring well, for 1 minute. Add milk, stirring with a whisk. Cook, stirring constantly, for 1 minute or until thick. Stir in heavy cream; cook, stirring, for 30 seconds. Add reserved spinach; cook, stirring, for 30 seconds or until thoroughly heated.

FOR THE PARMESAN WAFER

In a nonstick skillet, sprinkle Parmesan very evenly in about a 3-inch circle. Place skillet over low heat and watch carefully as liquid and grease slowly fry out and cheese becomes a very pale golden and crisp, about 3 to 5 minutes (too much color will produce a bitter flavor). With a thin spatula, very gently remove the wafer from the skillet and place on a flat surface. If desired, immediately cut wafer into a circle using a cookie cutter, tracing around the cutter with a knife if necessary. Allow wafer to cool completely. Insert wafer into a mound of creamed spinach as a garnish.

YIELD: 3–4 SERVINGS

CREAMED SPINACH

2 pounds fresh spinach, tough stems removed, washed well

2 tablespoons unsalted butter

2 teaspoons finely minced garlic

2 tablespoons flour

1 teaspoon salt

1 teaspoon freshly grated nutmeg

1 cup whole milk, heated

½ cup heavy cream

PARMESAN WAFER

1 tablespoon shredded Parmesan cheese for each serving of spinach

---

TIP | A good way to store leftover chunks of Parmesan cheese in your refrigerator is to wrap them in parchment paper and then in foil. It will preserve the flavor and texture better than plastic wrap will. —**Joachim Barrelman**, executive chef

Potatoes Gratinée

YIELD: 10 SERVINGS

2½ pounds potatoes

1 pint milk

1 pint heavy cream

Pinch of salt

Pinch of pepper

Pinch of nutmeg

1¼ cups grated Gruyère cheese
(about 5 ounces)

1¼ cups finely grated Parmesan
cheese (about 4 ounces)

¾ cup dry breadcrumbs

2 tablespoons snipped chives

6 tablespoons unsalted butter

Here we've taken classic potatoes gratinée and added Gruyère and Parmesan between the potato layers for extra flavor. For extra texture, we've covered the top with more cheese and a layer of crunchy breadcrumbs and chives. A wedge of these potatoes makes a stylish accompaniment.

Peel and wash potatoes and slice them into rounds ⅛-inch thick using a mandoline, the slicing disk of a food processor, or a sharp knife. Generously butter a 9-inch x 12-inch heavy shallow baking dish.

In a large saucepan, combine potatoes and milk and bring to a boil; simmer until potatoes are precooked but still firmly holding their shape. Add cream and season with salt, pepper, and nutmeg.

Preheat oven to 325°F. Layer potatoes in prepared baking dish, alternating layers with grated Gruyère and Parmesan. Finish with cheese on top. Sprinkle with breadcrumbs and chives and dot with butter.

Loosely cover with foil and bake potatoes for about 30 to 40 minutes, or until potatoes feel tender when pierced with a knife. Increase oven temperature to 425°F, remove foil, and bake until top is brown and crisp, about 10 minutes. Remove from oven and let rest a bit for liquids to absorb into potatoes. Cut into squares and serve.

TIP   To bring sophistication and geometric interest to the presentation of your dish, use a cookie cutter to cut circles from potatoes gratinée or serve rice that's been molded in a ramekin. Carrots are too often sliced into "coins"; shake things up by cutting them into matchsticks, thick sticks, or even cubes. —**Robert Hendrix**, executive chef

Savory Golden Rice

T his rice's golden hue and subtle spicing complements many meat, fish, and poultry dishes.

In a small heavy saucepan, heat 2 tablespoons butter over medium-low heat. Add onion, turmeric, and cardamom; cook, stirring, until onion is softened. Add rice and cook, stirring, until it is coated with butter. Add stock; bring liquid to a boil, cover, and reduce heat. Simmer mixture for 17 minutes, or until liquid is absorbed and rice is tender. Stir in the remaining 1 tablespoon butter; season with salt and pepper.

NOTE

To boost the flavors, color, and texture of this rice, right before serving stir in ⅓ cup toasted chopped almonds or pistachios, ⅓ cup soaked and drained golden raisins or dried cranberries, and ⅓ cup thinly sliced scallion greens.

YIELD: 2 SERVINGS

3 tablespoons unsalted butter

¾ cup finely chopped onion

¾ teaspoon turmeric

¼ teaspoon ground cardamom

1 cup long-grain rice

2 cups chicken stock, canned or homemade (see Pantry Staples)

Salt

Freshly ground black pepper

Creamy Polenta

P olenta adds a creamy contrast to many dishes. Or grill it or sauté it to add crispness of its own.

Coat an 11-inch x 7-inch baking dish with 1 tablespoon butter. In a heavy saucepan, bring chicken stock and remaining 1 tablespoon butter to a boil over high heat. Using a long-handled wooden spoon, stir stock constantly in one direction while adding cornmeal in a very slow stream by picking it up in handfuls and letting it run through your fingers. The process should take 4 to 5 minutes and the mixture will become harder and harder to stir as you add more cornmeal. Once cornmeal is incorporated, simmer, stirring constantly in the same direction, for about 20 to 30 minutes, or until polenta comes away from the sides of the pan. It's done when a spoon stands up when stuck in the middle.

Whisk in olive oil and cream (if using). Season with salt and pepper. Pour into prepared baking dish, cover with plastic wrap, and reserve. (Polenta will keep, covered, in the refrigerator for up to 2 days. Cut into squares and reheat by sautéing in butter, or brush with oil and grill.)

YIELD: 6–8 SERVINGS

2 tablespoons unsalted butter

1 quart chicken stock, canned or homemade (see Pantry Staples)

1 cup coarsely ground cornmeal

2 tablespoons extra-virgin olive oil

¼ cup heavy cream (optional)

Salt

Freshly ground black pepper

Classic Mashed Potatoes: Theme and Variations

YIELD: 4–6 SERVINGS

3 pounds Yukon gold potatoes (not peeled)

1½ cups whole milk or cream or a combination

¾ stick (6 tablespoons) unsalted butter

Salt

Freshly ground white or black pepper

These potatoes are boiled with their skins on, which adds nutrients and flavor; the skins are removed after cooking. If you wish to peel them first, cut the potatoes in half and watch them carefully because the cooking time will be less. Mashed potatoes are a superb canvas for flavor; the variations below are just a few suggestions.

In a 5-quart pot cover potatoes with cold salted water by 2 inches. Simmer until tender, 35 to 45 minutes. (The cooking time for the whole potatoes will depend on their size. Keep an eye on the pot; overcooking will make the potatoes crack open and break apart in the cooking water.) Meanwhile, in a small saucepan slowly warm milk (or cream) with butter over low heat until butter is melted. Remove pan from heat and keep milk mixture warm, covered.

In a colander, drain potatoes and cool just until they can be handled. Peel potatoes, transferring to a large bowl. Add three-fourths of the hot milk mixture. Season with salt and pepper. With a potato masher or electric hand mixer, mash or beat potatoes until smooth, adding more milk mixture if necessary to make them creamy (be careful not to beat too long or they may become gluelike). Serve immediately.

VARIATIONS

Garlic Mashed Potatoes: Simmer potatoes with 10 peeled garlic cloves. Mash cloves with the potatoes. For texture and even more flavor, sauté 2 cloves garlic thinly sliced over low heat in olive oil until tender (but not brown) and stir it into the mashed potatoes.

Basil Mashed Potatoes: After plating potatoes, very lightly swirl in some basil oil or basil pesto (see Pantry Staples) to create a marbling effect.

Mushroom Mashed Potatoes: Sauté shallots and thinly sliced cremini mushrooms and fold them into the mashed potatoes. After plating spoon some sautéed mushrooms on the top.

Bacon and Onion Potatoes: Right before serving, crumble 4 strips pan-fried bacon into mashed potatoes along with a chopped onion sautéed in some of the bacon drippings.

Horseradish Mashed Potatoes: Mash 3 tablespoons prepared horseradish into mashed potatoes. Serve with beef or salmon.

Mustard Mashed Potatoes: Add 3 tablespoons whole-grain or coarse-grain mustard to the potatoes along with the salt and pepper.

Cheddar/Broccoli Potatoes: Combine ½ cup grated cheddar cheese with 1 cup chopped, steamed broccoli florets, and fold the mixture into the mashed potatoes.

Red Coats: Substitute purple, red, or red-skinned new potatoes for the Yukon gold potatoes and leave their skins on when mashing.

Tatties 'n' Neeps: For this classic Scottish variation, combine equal amounts mashed potatoes and mashed turnips.

Colcannon: For St. Patrick's Day, add 1½ cups shredded cooked and drained cabbage or kale to the mashed potatoes. Make a well in the mound of potatoes on the plate and fill it with melted butter.

Scallion Mashed Potatoes: Mash potatoes with ¾ cup chopped scallions (with tender green portion), raw or sautéed in a little butter.

Herbed Mashed Potatoes: Substitute some compound butter for some of the butter in the recipe (see Tip in this chapter).

Smoked Salmon Mashed Potatoes: Substitute cream cheese for some of the butter when mashing, and then fold in 2 tablespoons snipped chives, 1 tablespoon chopped fresh dill, 2 tablespoons capers, and 4 ounces finely chopped smoked salmon. Serve with eggs Benedict.

Lobster Mashed Potatoes: Boil 1 or 2 lobsters or lobster tails in salted water until meat is just opaque in center. Remove lobsters, let cool, and dice meat. Discard half the lobster cooking liquid, add more fresh water, and use this water to cook peeled, halved potatoes. Drain and mash the potatoes (use milk rather than cream). Fold in lobster meat.

Mashed Sweet Potatoes: Peel 1½ pounds sweet potatoes and slice into ⅛-inch slices. Cook in a vegetable steamer for 15 to 18 minutes until soft and mash with 2 teaspoons minced fresh thyme, ⅛ teaspoon salt, and ⅛ teaspoon freshly ground black pepper.

TIP | Roll leftover mashed potatoes into a long log shape; wrap the log in plastic and refrigerate overnight. The next day, slice the roll into ½-inch patties and fry them in butter. It's a quick and delicious hash brown. If you want to get slightly fancier about it, dredge the potato patties in beaten egg before frying. —**Peter Lontoc,** executive chef

NOTE

An easy way to keep mashed potatoes hot on a buffet is to serve them from a crock pot at the lowest setting (stir every once in a while) or from an insulated ice bucket.

Mushroom Brochette

YIELD: 2–3 SERVINGS

10 ounces button mushrooms, wiped clean

2 tablespoons unsalted butter

Salt

Freshly ground black pepper

3 long sprigs fresh rosemary

his vegetable garnish came about because I wanted to keep the sautéed mushrooms from rolling around on the plate. I put a rosemary skewer through them and voilà! Problem solved.

Remove stems from mushrooms and save for another use, such as for stock or stuffing. In a large nonstick skillet, heat butter over medium-high heat. Add mushroom caps and cook, stirring, until seared but still plump. Season with salt and pepper and remove from the heat. Let cool slightly.

Remove most of the leaves from the rosemary sprigs, leaving a few at one end. Skewer 6 mushroom caps onto each stem, grouping caps of similar size together. To serve, reheat skewered mushrooms in a sauté pan with butter or in a warm oven. Serve immediately.

Baby Carrots and Asparagus

YIELD: 6 SERVINGS

2 pounds baby carrots with tops

1½ pounds thin asparagus

2 tablespoons unsalted butter, softened

1 medium shallot, minced

Salt

Freshly ground black pepper

NOTE

As a variation, substitute a medium red onion for the shallot and toss finely minced fresh dill with the vegetables right before serving.

imple and elegant, these vegetables celebrate spring, and can give a colorful lift to late-winter stews or roasts. Substitute sugar snap peas for the asparagus, if you like.

Trim carrot tops to ⅛ inch and diagonally cut asparagus into spears the length of the carrots.

Cook carrots in boiling salted water until crisp-tender, about 3 to 4 minutes. Immediately transfer with a slotted spoon to paper towels to drain. Return water to a boil and cook asparagus until crisp-tender, about 2 minutes. Transfer to paper towels to drain.

Meanwhile, in a medium saucepan, heat butter over medium heat. Add shallot, stir once, and cover; reduce the heat and cook, lifting the lid to stir occasionally, for 3 minutes, until shallots are translucent.

Add reserved carrots and asparagus and cook, gently stirring, until just heated through. Season with salt and pepper. Divide among plates and serve immediately.

Sautéed Carrots

C arrots can take on many combinations of flavors and be all the better for it, and here we give three variations. Great with meats, chicken, and fish, these carrots are an easy enough everyday recipe but also make a lovely addition to even the most elegant Christmas Eve dinner.

Bring a medium saucepan of salted water to a boil. Prepare a medium bowl of ice water. Cook carrots in boiling salted water until crisp-tender, about 3 minutes. Immediately transfer with a slotted spoon to ice water; let cool and drain on paper towels.

Melt butter in a heavy large skillet over medium heat. If making recipe A, add garlic. For recipe B, add ginger; for recipe C, add paprika, onion, and garlic. Sauté for 1 minute. Mix in remaining ingredients for recipe A, B, or C. Add carrots and toss to heat through. Season with salt and pepper.

TIP Don't let leftover fresh herbs wither away in your refrigerator! Use them to make compound butters, which you can freeze for later use. Though usually placed atop just-grilled steak or fish as a sauce alternative, compound butter can liven up steamed vegetables, mashed potatoes, rice, risotto, and soup. To make, mix ½ stick softened butter with ½ teaspoon salt and freshly ground pepper to taste. Stir in flavorings, such as parsley, lemon juice, and lemon zest; minced shallot and minced fresh thyme; minced sun-dried tomato and basil; minced sage and finely chopped toasted walnuts; or minced shallot, minced garlic, and minced chervil and parsley. Once flavorings are mixed in, place flavored butter in the center of some plastic wrap; wrap it up and roll it into a cylinder shape, twisting the ends of the plastic wrap closed like a sausage. Refrigerate for up to 3 days or freeze for up to a month. Cut off slices as you need them. —**Raymond Southern**, executive chef

YIELD: 2 SERVINGS

CARROTS

4 large carrots, peeled, thinly sliced diagonally

2 tablespoons unsalted butter

A. LEMON AND HERB

1 teaspoon minced garlic

1½ teaspoons chopped fresh rosemary, dill, or thyme

1 teaspoon finely grated lemon zest

Fresh lemon juice, to taste

B. GINGER AND ORANGE

2 teaspoons minced fresh ginger

1 tablespoon chopped fresh parsley

1 teaspoon finely grated orange zest

Fresh orange juice to taste

C. PAPRIKA AND CAPERS

1 teaspoon sweet paprika

¼ cup minced onion

1 teaspoon minced garlic

1 tablespoon capers

1 tablespoon red wine vinegar

1 tablespoon chopped fresh parsley

Salt

Freshly ground black pepper

CHAPTER 12

DESSERTS & OTHER SWEET TREATS

At Holland America Line, we think of our meals as a breathtaking fireworks show—saving the most drama and unforgettable flair for the Big Finish. | On both land and sea, a fabulous dessert demonstrates the quality and artistic capabilities of a kitchen. Each Holland America Line ship has a head pastry chef, who has extensive training and experience and who is dedicated to the craft of making sweet works of art. His or her role is to ensure that the pastries are made to Holland America Line's high-quality specifications and are delivered to the table in an unforgettable presentation designed to impress our guests. | The head pastry chef has a team of chefs, each member of which has been hand-picked and trained in Holland America Line's own Culinary Training Center in the Philippines. These pastry chefs work about ten hours a day, starting at seven in the morning to prepare ingredients for lunch. They slice fresh fruit, prepare fresh pastry, and bake a myriad of cakes. As much work as can be accomplished in advance is completed so that during the actual mealtime, the pastry cooks can concentrate on preparing cooked-to-order desserts such as soufflés.

What makes a dessert truly fabulous is that it is as delicious as it is dramatic. That's the idea behind my signature dessert, Chef Rudi's Famous White Chocolate Toque Filled with Silky Bittersweet Chocolate Mousse, which literally has a signature inscribed in chocolate. But just as stunning

Delectable and easy-to-make, Classic Bread-and-Butter Pudding is a treat for everyone.

SEDUCTIVE CHOCOLATE MARTINI

Ramil Mulawan, bartender

This truly fabulous chocolate delivery system satisfies your cacao craving just when you need it to, but it's most often sipped after a meal—with or without dessert! You have a choice to use either white or dark crème de cacao.

2 ounces vanilla vodka

1 ounce white or dark crème de cacao

Espresso beans or chocolate curl for garnish (optional; see Note)

Fill a pint glass with ice. Add vanilla vodka and crème de cacao. Cap with shaker can and shake vigorously. Strain into a chilled martini glass. Garnish with chocolate curl or espresso beans.

YIELD: 1 DRINK

NOTE: To make a chocolate curl, place finely chopped semisweet chocolate into the top of a double boiler placed over barely simmering (not boiling) water. Just when chocolate is melted, remove top of boiler and place it on a folded kitchen towel to blot any drops of steam from its underside. Immediately pour chocolate onto a marble slab or any clean, washable surface. Allow chocolate to set. Using a cheese cutter, rake over chocolate to form long individual curls.

MICHEL BERHOCOIRIGOIN
Corporate executive pastry chef

CHEF'S NOTE FROM THE GALLEY

When making fresh whipped cream, rather than using granulated sugar to sweeten it, try using confectioners' sugar instead. The resulting whipped cream will be fluffier, stay firmer, and will never have any of the grittiness that can occur when making whipped cream with regular sugar.

and popular is the Holland America Line Bread-and-Butter Pudding, which is served in the Lido restaurants of our ships. This particular dessert must be available every single day. It's so good and is such a beloved tradition for Holland America Line, that our guests seek it out on a daily basis.

I always say to my culinary staff and students that the last four minutes of any meal is the most important. And I'll say it to you: for your desserts, use the finest ingredients and then think about giving the dish a memorable and distinctive presentation, whether it is the Seductive Chocolate Martini (a recipe from our amazing beverage department) or something more homey like the Dutch Apple Cake. Great visual appeal and attention to detail—such as an artfully sliced strawberry or a well-placed fresh vanilla bean—can make a great dessert taste even better.

Classic Bread-and-Butter Pudding

YIELD: 8 SERVINGS

1½ pounds good-quality day-old sliced white bread, crusts trimmed and slices cut into cubes

6 tablespoons unsalted butter, melted

1 quart whole milk

6 eggs, beaten

3 egg yolks, beaten

¾ cup sugar

1 teaspoon vanilla extract

¾ cup raisins

Confectioners' sugar, for sprinkling

NOTE

Try soaking the raisins in a little rum or cognac for 30 minutes before adding them. Or, instead of raisins, substitute dried cherries and chocolate chips.

T his custardy confection keeps you coming back for more, bite after nostalgic bite. Individual baking dishes add sophistication, but you can also bake it in a larger pan.

Preheat oven to 325°F. Butter 8 ramekins with 12-ounce capacity or a 9-inch x 13-inch baking dish. Have on hand a roasting pan large enough to hold the ramekins or baking dish, and line it with a folded kitchen towel.

Place bread cubes in a bowl. Drizzle and toss with melted butter. Spread out on a baking sheet and toast in the oven, stirring once, until lightly golden, about 8 to 10 minutes.

In a saucepan, bring milk to a simmer over medium heat. Meanwhile, in a large bowl whisk whole eggs, egg yolks, and sugar until blended. Gradually whisk in hot milk. Stir in vanilla.

TO ASSEMBLE

Divide half the bread cubes among prepared ramekins (or layer in prepared baking dish). Top with half the raisins. Cover with remaining bread cubes and raisins. Ladle custard evenly over bread cubes and raisins. Let stand until some custard is absorbed, about 20 minutes.

TO BAKE

Bring a large kettle of water to a boil. Place ramekins or baking dish in roasting pan and transfer to oven. Add enough boiling water to pan to reach halfway up side of ramekins (or baking dish). Bake puddings in middle of oven for 45 minutes, or until puffed and just set. Carefully remove roasting pan from oven and remove dishes. Let cool slightly and serve while still warm, sprinkled with confectioners' sugar.

TIP | Thoroughly creaming butter and sugar is a vital step for successful cakes and desserts. Most of the air bubbles in a cake are created in the creaming step—leaveners such as baking powder only enlarge bubbles already in the dough. For proper creaming, butter should be at a starting temperature of 65°F and mixing should last 5 to 8 minutes for a standing mixer and several minutes longer than that for a hand-held mixer. If the heat generated by the mixer starts to melt the butter, dip the bottom of the bowl in some ice water to cool it down. —**Dennis Starch**, executive chef

Trio of Crème Brûlées

A thin, sheer, burnt-sugar shell crowns these custards, flavored in three ways (vanilla, coffee, and chocolate) for those who simply can't decide which to choose. Make the custards one or two days ahead and caramelize the sugared top an hour or so before serving.

YIELD: 9 SERVINGS

3 cups heavy cream

1 cup milk

½ cup sugar

½ vanilla bean, split lengthwise

8 egg yolks

1½ ounces bittersweet (not unsweetened) chocolate, finely chopped

2 teaspoons coffee extract

9 tablespoons packed light brown sugar

Preheat oven to 250°F. Line a roasting pan with a folded kitchen towel. Place nine 4-ounce soufflé dishes or ramekins in roasting pan.

In a heavy medium saucepan, combine cream, milk, and ¼ cup sugar. With the tip of a blunt knife, scrape in seeds from vanilla bean; add bean. Slowly bring mixture to a boil over medium-low heat. Remove cream mixture from heat. Cover and steep 30 minutes, until vanilla has infused mixture.

In a mixing bowl, whisk remaining ¼ cup sugar and egg yolks until pale colored. Pour vanilla-infused cream into egg yolk mixture, whisking until well blended. Return mixture to saucepan. Cook custard over medium-low heat, stirring constantly with a wooden spoon, for 3 minutes (do not let custard boil). Strain custard into 3 clean bowls, dividing mixture equally among them. Immediately add chocolate to 1 bowl, stirring until melted. Stir coffee extract into another bowl. Leave third bowl as is.

Bring a large kettle of water to a boil. Ladle cream mixtures into ramekins, 3 of each flavor. Add boiling water to pan up to a depth of 1 inch. Bake custards for 1 hour, or until center moves only slightly when ramekin is touched. Carefully remove ramekins from pan; cool completely on a wire rack. Cover and chill for at least 4 hours or overnight.

Preheat broiler. Place brown sugar in a medium sieve and sprinkle it over custards. Place custard dishes on baking sheet. Broil until sugar is brown and caramelized, rotating baking sheet to broil evenly and watching closely to avoid burning, 1 to 2 minutes. (An alternative: hold a small kitchen blowtorch about 2 inches from the top of each custard and heat sugar, moving the torch back and forth, until sugar is completely melted and caramelized, about 1 minute.) Chill custards for 1 hour so sugar topping hardens. Serve.

NOTE

A kitchen blowtorch is essential if you plan to make crème brûlée often. The heat is easier to control than a broiler, and you are less likely to burn the crust. You can even use it to crisp the brown sugar on your morning bowl of oatmeal! An alternative is to make the brown sugar topping on the stovetop. In a small heavy saucepan, combine ¼ cup sugar and 1 tablespoon water over medium heat. Cook, without stirring, for 5 to 8 minutes or until golden. Immediately pour syrup evenly over cold custards and spread it to form a thin layer.

TIP

Brown sugar hard as a rock again? Place a slice of bread in the package with the sugar and seal it up again tightly. The sugar will absorb the moisture from the bread and soften the sugar up after a few hours. —**Ronald Waasdorp**, executive chef

Chef Rudi's Famous White Chocolate Toque Filled with Silky Bittersweet Chocolate Mousse

12 ounces fine-quality white chocolate, chopped

11 ounces fine-quality bittersweet (not unsweetened) chocolate, chopped

¼ cup plus 2 tablespoons whole milk

3 egg yolks

½ cup sugar

1 tablespoon Grand Marnier

1 tablespoon brandy or cognac

Finely grated zest from 1 orange

1 pint heavy cream

Mint sprigs, for garnish

Candied orange zest, for garnish (optional; see Pantry Staples)

Strawberries, raspberries, and/or blueberries, for garnish (optional)

Chocolate sauce, for garnish (optional)

This unique and sophisticated mousse-filled chef's hat—a Rudi Sodamin original!—demonstrates Holland America Line's Signature of Excellence initiative. I've provided instructions for making the mousse in delicate white chocolate cups, although the mold can be purchased through the company's website. Remember to garnish like a chef!

FOR THE WHITE CHOCOLATE CUPS

Line 10 muffin cups with standard-sized (2½-inch diameter) foil or paper liners. Melt white chocolate in top of double boiler placed over (not touching) simmering water, stirring until smooth. Spoon 1 tablespoon melted white chocolate into each liner. With a pastry brush, brush chocolate over bottom and up sides of liners to coat evenly (brush all the way to the top but not over the edge.) You want most of the chocolate on the sides; try not to get too thick a layer on the bottom or where the bottom and sides join. Freeze until chocolate firms, about 30 minutes.

Re-melt remaining white chocolate; add 1 tablespoon to each cup and brush over bottom and up sides, forming second coat. Freeze until completely set, about 1 hour. (Can be made 1 day ahead. Cover; keep frozen.)

When chocolate is set, line a baking sheet with waxed paper. Working quickly but gently, pick up 1 cup and carefully begin to peel the liner from the set chocolate cup without holding the chocolate cup (or any section of it) in your hands any longer than necessary. When liner is peeled off, place chocolate cup on lined baking sheet. Repeat peeling with other cups. Cover airtight, and store in a single layer in the refrigerator until needed.

FOR THE MILK CHOCOLATE MOUSSE

Place bittersweet chocolate in a bowl. In a small saucepan, bring milk to a boil. Immediately pour over chocolate, stirring until smooth. Cool briefly. Meanwhile, combine egg yolks and sugar in large metal bowl. Set bowl over (not touching) simmering water in base of double boiler and whisk until mixture is frothy and candy thermometer registers 160°F, about 6 minutes. Remove from hot water.

Using an electric mixer, beat yolk mixture until thick and cool, about 3 minutes. Fold slightly cooled chocolate into yolk mixture. Stir in Grand Marnier, brandy or cognac, and grated orange zest. Beat cream in medium bowl until stiff peaks form. Fold into chocolate mixture in 3 additions. Cover and refrigerate for at least 1 hour.

Place white chocolate cups on plates. Using a piping bag with a decorative tip, pipe mousse into cups (you will have leftover mousse). Let sit for 10 minutes so that chocolate cups will be softer to eat. Garnish with mint, candied orange zest, berries, and chocolate sauce, as desired. Serve immediately.

Warm Grand Marnier Chocolate Volcano Cake

The soft, puddinglike center of these individual cakes, famous in our Pinnacle Grill, keeps customers cheering for more. Enjoy this rich cake as is or with a scoop of vanilla ice cream on top.

Preheat oven to 375°F. Butter eight 6-ounce soufflé dishes or custard cups (see Note).

Place chocolate and 2 sticks (8 ounces) butter in top of double boiler placed over (not touching) 1 inch of simmering water. Whisk until chocolate is smooth. Remove from hot water and let mixture cool to lukewarm.

Meanwhile, in a large mixing bowl, combine remaining 1 stick (4 ounces) butter and ⅓ cup sugar. With an electric mixer, beat at medium speed until light and fluffy. One by one add 2 whole eggs and 3 egg yolks (reserve egg whites), beating for a full 30 seconds after each addition. Add lukewarm chocolate mixture, beating until combined. On low speed, stir in Grand Marnier, vanilla, and orange zest until just incorporated.

In a medium bowl, sift flour, cocoa powder, baking powder, and salt. Beat flour mixture into chocolate mixture at low speed until just incorporated. Increase speed to high and beat for 3 minutes, stopping 2 or 3 times to scrape down the sides of the bowl.

Place the remaining 3 egg whites in a clean, grease-free mixing bowl. With clean beaters, beat on low speed until frothy. Increase speed to medium and gradually add the remaining ⅓ cup sugar. When sugar is incorporated, increase speed to medium-high and beat until whites hold stiff but not dry peaks. With a rubber spatula, fold egg whites into chocolate mixture until well combined.

Divide mixture among prepared soufflé dishes and place on baking sheet. Bake until cakes are firm around edges but a nickel-size area in the center still moves slightly when shaken, about 9 to 12 minutes (do not overbake). Remove from oven and let cool for at least 5 minutes. Serve in the dishes, with any optional garnishes as desired.

NOTE

Baking time will vary depending on the volume capacity of the soufflé dishes you use and their depth or shallowness. If you only have 4-ounce capacity dishes, baking time could be as little as 5 minutes. Dishes up to 12 ounces in capacity may take as much as 25 minutes. You can use what you have on hand for this recipe, but keep a watchful eye on the cakes and check them as they bake.

YIELD: 8 SERVINGS

8 ounces fine-quality bittersweet (not unsweetened) chocolate

3 sticks (12 ounces) unsalted butter

⅔ cup sugar

5 eggs, 2 whole and 3 separated

2 tablespoons Grand Marnier

1 tablespoon vanilla

Finely grated zest of 2 oranges

¾ cup flour

3 tablespoons cocoa powder

2 teaspoons baking powder

Pinch of salt

Garnish cookies (optional; see Pantry Staples)

Whipped cream, for garnish (optional)

Candied orange zest, for garnish (optional; see Pantry Staples)

Mango-Banana-Pistachio Strudel with Raspberry Sauce and Dried Mango Chips

YIELD: 6 SERVINGS

STRUDEL

½ cup shelled pistachio nuts

4 sheets phyllo dough
(18 inches x 14 inches)

1 stick unsalted butter, melted

2 tablespoons sugar

½ cup yellow or white cake crumbs

3 ripe bananas, peeled and split
lengthwise

1 large mango, peeled, pitted, and
chopped into ¼-inch dice

Confectioners' sugar, for sprinkling

MANGO CHIPS

3 tablespoons confectioners' sugar

1 mango, unpeeled and well washed

RASPBERRY SAUCE

2 (12-ounce) packages frozen
unsweetened raspberries, thawed

⅔ cup sugar

¼ cup water

1 tablespoon kirsch or framboise
liqueur (optional)

C hase away the wintertime blues with this exciting combination of creamy tropical fruit in crisp phyllo. You can make the mango chips and raspberry sauce up to two days in advance.

FOR THE STRUDEL

Preheat oven to 350°F. Spread pistachios on a baking sheet and bake for 5 to 7 minutes. Let cool, chop, and set aside. Increase oven temperature to 375°F. Lightly coat baking sheet with butter.

Lay 1 sheet of phyllo on a work surface. (Keep remaining phyllo covered with a damp kitchen towel and plastic wrap.) With a pastry brush, brush phyllo sheet lightly with some melted butter. Sprinkle with one-fourth of sugar and one-fourth of cake crumbs. Lay another sheet of phyllo on top. Lightly brush with more butter and sprinkle with more sugar and cake crumbs. Repeat with remaining 2 sheets of phyllo.

Arrange some sliced bananas and diced mango along 1 long edge of phyllo so that bananas cover an 18-inch x 3-inch area. Sprinkle fruit with some pistachios. Top fruit with remaining bananas, mango, and pistachios.

Starting from the fruit-lined edge, roll up phyllo into a cylinder. Place strudel on prepared baking sheet and brush with melted butter. Bake for 10 minutes, or until pastry is golden crisp on the outside and warm on the inside.

FOR THE MANGO CHIPS

Preheat oven to 200°F. Line a large baking sheet with parchment paper, nonstick foil, or a nonstick baking pad. Sift 1½ tablespoons confectioners' sugar evenly onto lined baking sheet. Use your palm to hold down a whole mango as you make slices around the pit with a mandoline or other manual slicer. Keep fingers clear. Arrange a single layer of the best-looking slices on the prepared baking sheet and sprinkle evenly with remaining 1½ tablespoons confectioners' sugar. Bake slices in middle of oven until beginning to crisp, about 2 hours. Immediately peel chips off parchment and cool on a rack.

FOR THE RASPBERRY SAUCE

In a heavy medium saucepan, stir berries, sugar, and water over medium heat until mixture just comes to a boil, stirring occasionally. Transfer mixture to food processor and purée. Scrape into a wire mesh strainer set over bowl; press on solids to extract as much liquid as possible; discard solids in strainer. Mix liqueur into sauce, if desired. Thin with water if necessary.

TO SERVE

Transfer strudel to a cutting board and slice into 6 diagonal slices. Sprinkle with confectioners' sugar and transfer to plates. Garnish with fruit sauce and mango chips.

DESSERTS & OTHER SWEET TREATS 167

Double Fudge Chocolate Avalanche Cake with Grand Marnier Whipped Cream and Berry Sauce

T his over-the-top dessert proves you can't have too much of a good thing. That's why we call it avalanche cake! Grab a big fork (or some ski poles) and "tuck in."

FOR THE CAKE

Preheat oven to 350°F. Butter and flour two 15½-inch x 10½-inch x 1-inch jelly roll pans or two 9-inch x 13-inch baking pans.

In a large bowl, sift together flour, cocoa powder, baking powder, salt, baking soda, and cinnamon; set aside.

In another large bowl, combine butter and sugar. With an electric mixer, beat at medium-high speed until pale and fluffy, 5 to 8 minutes. Add eggs 1 at a time, beating well after each addition. Reduce speed to low and beat in reserved dry ingredients in 3 additions, alternately, with milk in 2 additions.

Divide batter among prepared pans. Smooth tops. Bake until firm in center when lightly pressed and toothpick inserted in center comes out clean, about 40 minutes. Cool in pan on wire rack until room temperature, at least 1 hour.

FOR THE FUDGE FILLING

Finely chop chocolate and place in a medium mixing bowl. In a small saucepan, bring cream and milk to a boil over moderately low heat. Pour cream mixture over chocolate, whisking until chocolate is melted. Let cool to room temperature.

Cut butter into pieces and add to chocolate mixture. With an electric mixer, beat fudge filling until smooth, about 5 minutes.

TO SERVE

Run a thin knife around edges of 1 pan and invert layer onto a cardboard base. Spread with filling. Top with second cake layer and spread more filling over top and sides. Cut cake into squares and place on serving plates. Top each square with generous dollops of flavored whipped cream. Decorate with sweetened berries and their juices and Garnish Cookies, if desired.

YIELD: 20 SERVINGS

CAKE

3¼ cups flour

1 cup cocoa powder

1 tablespoon plus 1 teaspoon baking powder

2½ teaspoons salt

2 teaspoons baking soda

1 teaspoon ground cinnamon

2 sticks unsalted butter (8 ounces), softened

3½ cups sugar

7 eggs

2 cups milk

FUDGE FILLING

1 pound fine-quality bittersweet (not unsweetened) chocolate

½ cup heavy cream

¼ cup plus 2 tablespoons milk

1 stick unsalted butter (4 ounces), softened slightly

GARNISHES

1 quart heavy cream whipped with ½ cup sugar and then flavored with ¼ cup Grand Marnier

4 cups fresh berries (blueberries, raspberries, blackberries, and/or halved strawberries) tossed with ½ cup sugar and chilled for 2 hours

Garnish Cookies in jagged shape (optional; see Pantry Staples)

Dutch Apple Cake

APPLE FILLING

3¼ pounds baking apples (about 11)

¼ cup plus 2 tablespoons cornstarch

¾ cup sugar

½ teaspoon salt

⅔ cup water

1 teaspoon cinnamon

Pinch of nutmeg

¾ cup raisins

SWEET PASTRY

2 sticks unsalted butter (½ pound), softened slightly

½ cup sugar

1 egg, beaten

1 tablespoon vanilla extract

½ teaspoon salt

2¾ cups flour

Crème anglaise (optional; see Pantry Staples)

ore like a pie than a cake, this traditional Dutch confection features a juicy heap of sliced apples and raisins baked in a sweet and buttery crust with a lattice top.

FOR THE APPLE FILLING

Peel and core apples. Slice ¼-inch thick and place in a large bowl. In a small bowl, whisk cornstarch, sugar, and salt; set aside.

In a medium saucepan, bring ⅔ cup water to a boil. Whisk in reserved cornstarch mixture and reduce heat to medium-low. Cook, stirring constantly, until sugar is dissolved and mixture is thick. Scrape cornstarch mixture over apples and toss to coat well. Add cinnamon, nutmeg, and raisins, and stir to combine; let cool completely. (Filling can be refrigerated, covered, up to a day in advance.)

FOR THE SWEET PASTRY

In the bowl of an electric mixer, combine butter and sugar. Beat on medium speed until light and fluffy, about 2 minutes. Pour in half the beaten egg (reserve remainder) and beat until combined, scraping down the sides of the bowl. Beat in vanilla and salt.

With a wooden spoon, stir in flour until combined. Do not overmix. Gather dough into ball, kneading with your hand until it comes together; divide into 2 pieces, 1 slightly larger than the other. Flatten larger piece into disk and smaller piece into rectangle; wrap each in plastic and refrigerate for at least 3 hours. (Can be made 1 day ahead; keep refrigerated. Let soften slightly at room temperature before rolling out.)

TO ASSEMBLE

Preheat oven to 400°F. Butter a 9-inch round springform cake pan, or spray it with nonstick spray. Roll out larger piece of dough (disk) onto floured surface to ¼-inch thick. (If your pan is 3 inches deep, circle will need to be 15 inches in diameter.) Ease crust into bottom and up sides of prepared pan, patching as necessary. Leave a ½-inch overhang.

Spoon apple filling into crust. Roll out dough rectangle until it is less than ¼-inch thick. Cut lengthwise into twelve ½-inch-wide strips. Place 6 strips 1-inch apart atop apple filling. Place remaining 6 strips diagonally atop first 6 strips, forming diamond lattice pattern. Trim strips even with bottom crust. Fold dough overhang in, pressing onto edge of cake pan. Press dough edge to seal.

Brush dough strips with remaining beaten egg. Bake cake for 15 minutes. Reduce oven temperature to 350°F. Continue to bake until crust is golden and apples are tender, covering crust edges with foil if browning too quickly, about 1 hour longer. Cool at least 2 hours. Remove side of pan and serve cake slightly warm or at room temperature with crème anglaise, if desired.

TIP | Do not add cold eggs straight from the refrigerator to creamed butter and sugar. If your eggs are cold when you need to use them, warm them in their shells in a bowl of hot tap water first. —**Guenther Cussigh**, corporate executive chef

CHAPTER 13

PANTRY STAPLES

Usually when a cookbook includes a chapter called Pantry Staples, it will have a handful of fundamental recipes for basic rouxs, doughs, and stocks. But that's not what you will find in this chapter. | On a ship, the word pantry means something more than the cupboard full of basic ingredients that the word connotes. In fact, we have a cold pantry and a hot pantry. | Online or in many cookbooks, you can find recipes for basics such as chicken stock and beef stock, and you will find some of them here, too; they are fundamental to good cooking (though in a pinch, it would be a shame not to reach for an excellent-quality ready-made product—so many of which are available at stores— that will allow you to focus on more adventurous parts of a recipe).

ULTRA STRAWBERRY LEMONADE

Alvin Angeles, bartender

Definitely not your grandmother's strawberry lemonade, this bright and breezy libation is a poolside delight on a sunny day.

2 wedges lemon
1½ ounces citrus vodka
2 ounces homemade sour mix
1 ounce water
2 ounces strawberry purée (see Note)
1 slice strawberry, for garnish

In a pint glass, hand-press lemon wedges with a muddler. Fill glass with ice. Add vodka, sour mix, water, and strawberry purée. Cap with shaker can and shake vigorously. Pour back into pint glass and garnish rim with strawberry slice. Serve with a straw.

YIELD: 1 DRINK

N O T E : To make strawberry purée, wash, hull, and slice fresh ripe straw-berries and place in a blender. Purée until smooth.

PETER KOFLER
Executive chef

To preserve unused fresh herbs, wrap them in a damp—but not soaked—paper towel, then place them in a plastic bag in the refrigerator. You can keep herbs about twice as long this way; it also keeps them from getting soggy, limp, or dried out along the edges.

CHEF'S NOTE FROM THE GALLEY

But to keep our menus fresh and exciting, and to be able to offer our guests what's beyond the shelves of even the most exclusive specialty food shops, our chefs are constantly creating dressings, sauces, and salsas. This is the work of our cold pantry—also known as a cold kitchen. When I think of pantry staples, I'm thinking of the sauces, salsas, or sides I can create that will turn a simple piece of grilled fish into something exquisite.

This pondering, dreaming, and flexing of creative muscles is fleet-wide. It is a signature aspect of the Holland America Line to take even the most basic offerings and transform them into something special, above predictable standards and expectations, and to make them truly memorable and remarkable taste experiences.

Start thinking of your pantry as your palette of paints from which to turn the blank canvas of your basic foods—salads, fish or chicken, or even hamburgers—into special dishes.

A TASTE OF EXCELLENCE

Homemade Sour Mix

Customers notice the difference that comes from using Holland America Line's fresh sour mix, made from scratch every day.

FOR THE SIMPLE SYRUP

In a large heavy pan, combine sugar and water. Bring to a boil, stirring to dissolve the sugar. Boil for 2 minutes. Remove from the heat and let cool. Transfer to a clean bottle or container and chill, covered, until needed. (Simple syrup can be made in any quantity you need by combining 1 part sugar and 1 part water and following the instructions above. It may be made 2 weeks ahead and chilled, covered.)

FOR THE SOUR MIX

In a jar with a lid, combine simple syrup and lime juice or lemon juice, depending on the overall flavor desired for the drink you're making. Cover and refrigerate for up to 2 weeks, or store in the freezer. (The fresher the sour mix, the fresher tasting your drink will be. It is most ideal if you can combine the simple syrup and juice in the quantity you need right before you start to make your drinks.)

YIELD: 2 CUPS

SIMPLE SYRUP

4 cups sugar

1 quart water

SOUR MIX

1 cup Simple Syrup (see above)

1 cup fresh lime juice or lemon juice

Tomato Salsa

Here is your classic tomato salsa recipe. Seeding the jalapeño reduces the spiciness, but wear rubber gloves as you do it to keep the fiery oils from penetrating the skin on your fingers and potentially transferring to more sensitive body parts (such as your eyes).

In a nonreactive bowl, combine tomatoes, onion, chiles, cilantro, salt, and pepper. Stir and toss well. Season with lime juice to taste. Let stand for 30 minutes before serving. (Salsa keeps, tightly covered, in the refrigerator for up to 2 days.)

YIELD: 1½ CUPS

4 medium tomatoes, peeled, seeded, and diced (see Tip, page 86)

1 small yellow onion, finely chopped

2 serrano or jalapeño chiles, stemmed, seeded, and finely chopped

2 tablespoons chopped fresh cilantro

½ teaspoon salt

Pinch of freshly ground black pepper

1 to 2 tablespoons fresh lime juice

Cranberry Cilantro Relish

YIELD: 2 CUPS

⅛ cup hazelnuts

1½ cups fresh cranberries

1 large navel orange, peeled, sectioned, and membranes removed

2 tablespoons dried cranberries

2 tablespoons chopped fresh cilantro leaves

1 tablespoon seeded and minced fresh poblano chile pepper

½ cup sugar

Not just for Thanksgiving anymore, this nutty, tart, and savory relish will pick up the beat of your favorite Southwestern-spiced poultry or pork.

In a dry skillet over high heat, stir hazelnuts, taking care not to scorch them, until pale golden beneath the skins. Let cool briefly, then rub inside a clean kitchen towel to remove as much of the skins as possible. Coarsely chop nuts and transfer them to a nonreactive bowl.

In a food processor, pulse fresh cranberries until coarsely chopped. Add them to nuts along with remaining ingredients; stir to combine. Cover and refrigerate until ready to use.

Avocado Salsa or Guacamole

YIELD: 1 CUP

1 ripe avocado, halved, pitted, and peeled

2 tablespoons chopped fresh cilantro (optional)

1 tablespoon finely diced red onion

1 tablespoon minced jalapeño, minus seeds (wear rubber gloves)

1 to 2 tablespoons fresh lime juice

Salt

Freshly ground black pepper

When flavoring avocado salsa or guacamole, it's important to remember not to obscure the avocado, but to enhance it. Use Haas avocado for guacamole; either Haas or Fuerte (with smooth green skin) works fine in the salsa.

If making avocado salsa, coarsely chop avocado and combine in a bowl with cilantro (if using), onion, and jalapeño. Season to taste with lime juice, salt, and pepper.

If making guacamole, mash together avocado, cilantro, onion, and jalapeño in a bowl with a fork until smooth. Season to taste with lime juice, salt, and pepper. (For a smoother guacamole, purée in a food processor, adding a little water if necessary.)

NOTE

Avocado salsa or guacamole can be made 1 hour ahead and chilled, its surface covered with plastic wrap.

Béarnaise Sauce

his French sauce brings classic elegance to meat, fish, eggs, and vegetables.

In a small saucepan, combine shallot, peppercorns, tarragon, and both vinegars. Bring to a boil and cook until almost evaporated. Remove from heat and add water.

Transfer tarragon mixture to a double boiler and whisk together with egg yolks. Place the double boiler over (but not touching) boiling water and whisk constantly until mixture forms thick ribbons.

While whisking constantly, add butter, little by little, waiting for each addition to be incorporated before adding any more, until sauce triples in volume. Do not overcook sauce; it should be warm but not hot. (You may need to remove the bowl from the water, from time to time, if the sauce gets too hot.)

Strain to remove any cooked egg particles, if necessary. Whisk in herbs and season with salt and pepper.

1 tablespoon chopped shallot

3 cracked black peppercorns

1 tablespoon dried tarragon

3 tablespoons tarragon vinegar

4 tablespoons white wine vinegar

5 tablespoons water

3 egg yolks

¾ cup clarified unsalted butter, warmed (see Note)

1 teaspoon coarsely chopped fresh tarragon

1 teaspoon coarsely chopped fresh chervil

Salt

Freshly ground black pepper

NOTE

To clarify butter, melt 1 cup unsalted butter in a medium saucepan over low heat. Cook until the butterfat becomes clear and milk solids drop to the bottom of the pan. Skim the surface foam as the butter separates. Carefully spoon the clear butterfat into a measuring cup. Discard the milky liquid at the bottom of the saucepan.

TIP | To check if a sauce is the right consistency, dip a spoon into it and then trace a clean finger across the back of the spoon. If the trail you made with your finger remains, the sauce is thick enough. —**Peter Lontoc,** executive chef

Crème Fraîche

YIELD: 3 CUPS

2 cups heavy cream
1½ cups sour cream

Tangy and nutty in flavor, velvety in texture, this versatile kitchen staple is used in both savory and sweet dishes, whether used on canapés or in soups or dolloped on warm apple crisp. Because it can be boiled without curdling, it's ideal for sauces, too.

In a small saucepan, heat heavy cream over low heat, stirring continuously, for approximately 6 minutes, until just lukewarm. Do not boil. Remove from heat.

In a medium mixing bowl, whisk sour cream until smooth, approximately 2 minutes. Add lukewarm heavy cream and whisk until well combined. Cover with a clean kitchen towel and let stand at room temperature (about 70°F) for 15 hours, or until thick.

Transfer mixture to a nonreactive container; cover and refrigerate overnight. (The crème fraîche will keep, covered, in the refrigerator for up to 10 days.)

Very Berry Sauce

YIELD: 2 CUPS

½ cup sugar
⅓ cup water
1 cup fresh blackberries
1 cup fresh raspberries
1 tablespoon fresh lemon juice

This simple sauce is perfect drizzled on a fresh fruit salad, but try any leftovers on waffles, angel food cake, cheesecake, or lemon gelato.

In a small saucepan, bring sugar and water to a boil, stirring until sugar is dissolved. Transfer to a blender. Add berries and lemon juice. Pulse until berries are chopped.

Place mixture in a wire sieve over a bowl. Using a ladle, push sauce through sieve, leaving seeds behind. Discard seeds. (Sauce may be stored, covered, in the refrigerator for up to 2 days.)

Garnish Cookies

C ut into interesting shapes or molded into curves, these delicate melt-in-your-mouth cookies can take a dessert from simple to sensational.

Preheat oven to 375°F. Line a baking sheet with parchment paper.

In a bowl, mix together egg whites, flour, and confectioners' sugar. Stir in melted butter and vanilla (do not overmix).

With a pastry brush, spread a very thin layer of mixture onto parchment paper. Bake until golden brown.

When still warm, cut dough into shapes or into lengthwise strips and remove from tray. If desired, place cookie around a coffee mug or glass to obtain a round design. Once cold, remove it.

YIELD: 12 PIECES

4 egg whites

1 cup flour

1 cup confectioners' sugar

4 tablespoons melted unsalted butter

1 teaspoon vanilla extract

Candied Orange Zest

E asy to make, candied orange zest brings a bright bite to baked goods and makes a beautiful garnish. It's delicious to nibble, too.

Remove zest from oranges with a vegetable peeler in long ½-inch-wide pieces. Cut pieces into matchsticks.

In a small saucepan, cover zest with water and bring to a boil. Simmer zest for 5 minutes and drain in a sieve, discarding liquid. Repeat procedure 2 more times.

Combine sugar, ¼ cup water, and zest in pan and bring to a boil over moderate heat. Simmer until liquid is reduced to a thick syrup. Cool orange zest in syrup. (Candied zest keeps, covered, in the refrigerator for up to 1 week.)

YIELD: ½ CUP

2 navel oranges

¼ cup sugar

¼ cup water

Crème Anglaise

⅔ cup half-and-half

½ vanilla bean, sliced open lengthwise

⅓ cup sugar

2 egg yolks

A traditional vanilla custard sauce, this can be served hot or cold over fruit, cake, or other desserts.

In a 1-quart saucepan, cook half-and-half and vanilla bean over medium heat until mixture just comes to a boil, about 3 to 5 minutes. Remove from heat; remove vanilla bean.

Meanwhile, whisk ⅓ cup sugar and egg yolks in small bowl until light and lemon-colored. Gradually add hot half-and-half in a stream, whisking, and return mixture to saucepan. Cook over medium heat, stirring constantly, until custard reaches 160°F, and is thick enough to leave a path on the back of the spoon when your finger is drawn across (2 to 3 minutes). Do not overcook.

Strain custard into a clean bowl and cool to warm. Cover and refrigerate at least 1 hour. (Crème anglaise can be stored, covered, in the refrigerator for up to 2 days.)

Green Goddess Dressing

1 cup (packed) watercress leaves

¾ cup sour cream or crème fraîche

⅓ cup light mayonnaise

2 tablespoons chopped scallions (include tender green portion)

2 tablespoons chopped fresh dill

1 tablespoon chopped fresh parsley

1 tablespoon chopped fresh tarragon

1 tablespoon chopped fresh mint

1 teaspoon fresh lemon juice

Salt

Freshly ground black pepper

Hot pepper sauce

This is a greener and more herbal rendition of the classic green goddess dressing. Use it on salads, fish, hard-boiled egg wedges, asparagus, roasted potatoes, and tomatoes. If you use ½ cup mayonnaise and ½ cup sour cream, it becomes a perfect dip for crudités.

Bring a saucepan of water to a boil. Prepare a bowl of ice water. Place watercress in boiling water for 30 seconds. With a sieve, transfer watercress to ice water to stop the cooking. Drain and pat dry with paper towels. Transfer watercress to a blender. Add sour cream, mayonnaise, scallions, herbs, and lemon juice. Blend until smooth. Transfer to a bowl and season with salt, pepper, and hot pepper sauce. (Dressing will keep, covered, in the refrigerator for up to 3 days.)

Tzaziki

YIELD: 3 CUPS

1 large English hothouse cucumber, peeled, halved lengthwise, and seeded

2 cups plain yogurt

1–2 tablespoons fresh lemon juice

4 cloves garlic, minced

2 tablespoons minced Italian parsley

½ teaspoon freshly ground black pepper

Pinch of kosher salt

¼ cup olive oil

Cucumber and yogurt sauce can transform leftover leg of lamb into an other-worldly experience. It's also a fantastic dip for pita bread or crudités.

Coarsely grate cucumber; place in a strainer and let stand at room temperature until most of the liquid drains out, about 3 hours. Discard liquid. Pat dry to remove excess moisture.

In a nonreactive bowl, combine yogurt, lemon juice, garlic, parsley, pepper, and salt. Stir until blended. Gradually whisk in olive oil in a thin stream. Add reserved cucumber and stir to combine. Adjust seasoning. Cover and refrigerate for at least 1 hour and preferably overnight, to allow flavors to blend.

NOTE

For an even thicker dip, place yogurt in a strainer lined with 3 layers of cheesecloth over a large bowl. Let drain at room temperature for 3 hours. Discard liquid and use the thick yogurt for the recipe.

Pesto Sauce

YIELD: 1½ CUPS

1 clove garlic, or to taste

½ teaspoon salt

5 cups packed fresh basil leaves, rinsed

½ cup olive oil

½ cup grated Asiago, Parmesan, or Romano cheese

Made without cheese, the basil purée can be frozen; add cheese once it has defrosted.

In a food processor, combine garlic and salt. Pulse to chop. Add basil and oil. Pulse mixture until it is finely puréed but not a smooth paste.

Remove mixture from processor and transfer it to a bowl. Taste for seasoning and stir in another clove of finely chopped garlic, if desired.

If using immediately, stir in cheese. Otherwise, transfer pesto to a plastic container, cover tightly, and refrigerate. Stir in cheese just before serving.

Caesar Dressing

YIELD: 4 SERVINGS

2 cloves garlic

2 tablespoons fresh lemon juice

3 tablespoons extra virgin olive oil

3 anchovy fillets, drained,
or 1 teaspoon anchovy paste

2 teaspoons Dijon mustard

½ teaspoon Worcestershire sauce

⅓ cup mayonnaise

Salt

Here is a creamy version of the dressing made famous by Italian-born chef Caesar Cardini in Tijuana, Mexico, in 1924. Use it on romaine lettuce or toss it with cooked potatoes for a wonderful potato salad.

In a blender, combine all the ingredients except mayonnaise and salt. Blend until smooth. Add mayonnaise and pulse just to blend. Season with salt. Transfer to a container. Cover and refrigerate until ready to use.

Basil Oil

YIELD: 1 CUP

½ cup densely packed basil leaves

1 cup neutral oil, such as grape seed
or canola

Dot your plates with this intensely flavored oil, or use a few drops in a vinaigrette or to toss with pasta. Basil oil is also delicious swirled into steaming mashed potatoes.

Bring a large pot of salted water to a boil. Prepare a bowl of ice water. Drop basil leaves into boiling water and cook just until tender but still green, 2 to 3 minutes. Drain and immediately transfer leaves to ice water. When cool, squeeze out as much water as possible from basil and place in a food processor with a bit of the oil. With the machine running, add remaining oil in a slow steady stream. When oil is completely incorporated, transfer to a container, cover, and chill until needed. (Basil oil keeps, covered, for up to 1 week in the refrigerator.)

NOTE

If you want a more refined basil oil, use a blender instead of a food processor. When oil is completely incorporated, pour mixture through a cheesecloth-lined sieve placed over a bowl. Cover with plastic and let mixture drip overnight into bowl. Next day, transfer contents of bowl to a bottle and seal tightly.

Asian Vinaigrette

YIELD: 1¼ CUPS

¼ cup soy sauce

¼ cup fresh lime juice

¼ teaspoon finely grated lime zest

1 tablespoon grated fresh ginger

1 small clove garlic, minced

¾ cup peanut or canola oil

½ teaspoon sugar

Salt

Freshly ground white pepper to taste

Serve with mixed baby Asian greens, such as tatsoi, mustard, mizuna, and pea shoots. Or drizzle over steamed baby bok choy.

In a nonreactive bowl, combine soy sauce, lime juice and zest, ginger, and garlic. Slowly whisk in oil. Stir in sugar and season with salt and pepper. Cover and refrigerate until ready to use.

Vegetable Stock

YIELD: 9 CUPS

3 tablespoons unsalted butter

2 onions, peeled and chopped

2 leeks, white and pale green parts only, washed and chopped

2 carrots, peeled and chopped

2 stalks celery, chopped

¼ pound mushrooms, chopped

1 large potato, thinly sliced

1 medium turnip or parsnip, coarsely chopped

⅓ cup, plus 12 cups water

¼ cup lentils

4 cloves garlic, unpeeled

½ teaspoon black peppercorns

6 sprigs fresh thyme

1 bay leaf

12 parsley stems

1 teaspoon salt

Leagues apart from canned broth, you'll always want to keep some of this in your freezer. Depending on your plans for it, you can also add a chopped tomato and enrich the flavor with any chopped roasted summer vegetables, such as red bell pepper, fennel, and zucchini.

In a stockpot, heat butter over moderate heat. Add onions, stirring, and cook until tender. Add leeks, carrots, celery, mushrooms, potato, turnip (or parsnip), and ⅓ cup water. Simmer mixture, covered, stirring occasionally, for 5 minutes.

Add remaining water and remaining ingredients; bring to a boil, reduce heat, and simmer, uncovered, for 1 hour. Strain stock through a fine sieve into a bowl and let cool. Cover and refrigerate until needed.

Chicken Stock

YIELD: 2 QUARTS

4 pounds chicken bones and parts (backs, necks, carcasses, thighs)

3 quarts cold water

2 medium onions, coarsely chopped

2 carrots, cut into ½-inch chunks

2 stalks celery, cut into ½-inch chunks

1 leek, white and light green parts only, washed and cut into ½-inch chunks

3 sprigs parsley, with stems

3 sprigs thyme

6 whole black peppercorns

Regularly making chicken stock can become second nature to you, if you accumulate chicken bones and trimmings in your freezer over a couple of months.

Rinse chicken bones and parts well under cold running water and place them in a stockpot. Add cold water and slowly bring to a boil, uncovered, over medium-low heat. Reduce heat to very low and simmer very gently, with just a few bubbles at the edges, for 4 hours. Use a slotted spoon or ladle to skim the surface froth and foam occasionally.

Add the remaining ingredients to stock and simmer for 1 hour more. Turn off heat and let stock cool down, uncovered, for 30 minutes.

Using tongs or a slotted spoon, carefully remove bones from stock and discard them. Strain stock through a fine sieve into a clean metal container and discard vegetables left behind. For a very clear stock, strain stock again, this time through a fine sieve lined with several layers of cheesecloth.

If not using stock immediately, place metal container in cold ice water bath. Stir the liquid regularly as it cools down. As stock cools, it may be necessary to drain out some of the water in the bath and replace it with some ice. The entire batch must be cooled down to 40°F.

Portion stock into containers and store them, covered, in the refrigerator for up to 7 days or in the freezer for up to 6 months. Skim fat from surface and bring to a full boil before using.

NOTE

To make a darker stock suitable for use in making brown sauces, roast chicken bones first before adding the cold water.

Beef Stock

H omemade beef stock is worth the effort, and tastes better in recipes than most canned broth.

Preheat oven to 400°F. Arrange shanks and onions in single layer in a large roasting pan. Roast, uncovered, for 1 hour, or until shanks are golden brown on all sides. Transfer shanks and onions to a large stockpot.

Add remaining ingredients to shanks in stockpot and pour in enough cold water to cover by 2 inches. Bring to a boil, uncovered, over medium-high heat. Reduce heat to very low and simmer very gently, with just a few bubbles at the edges, for 8 to 12 hours. Turn off heat and let stock cool down, uncovered, for 1 hour.

Using tongs or a slotted spoon, carefully remove shanks from stock and discard them. Line a fine sieve with several layers of cheesecloth. Using a ladle, carefully strain stock through sieve into a clean metal container.

If not using immediately, place metal container in cold ice water bath. Stir stock regularly as it cools down. As stock cools, it may be necessary to add more ice to the bath. The entire batch must be cooled down to 40°F.

Portion stock into containers and store them, covered, in the refrigerator for up to 7 days or in the freezer for up to 6 months. Skim fat from surface and bring to a full boil before using.

TIP Browning meat so it develops a rich-tasting brown coating involves complex reactions of sugars and proteins with heat. To properly brown meat for maximum flavor, use a skillet (not nonstick) that can take high heat, use enough fat to coat the skillet, and make sure that your meat is dry and at room temperature. Season the meat right before cooking, and add it to the pan without crowding. Too much meat in the pan lowers the temperature of the oil and pan too much, which causes the meat to release its juices and steam, rather than brown. Even if a recipe says to brown all the meat at once, if your pan isn't big enough to do that, brown it in batches instead. —Ian Thomson, executive chef

YIELD: 2 QUARTS

2 pounds meaty crosscut beef shanks (preferably 1-inch thick)

2 pounds meaty crosscut veal shanks (preferably 1-inch thick)

2 medium onions, cut into chunks

2 carrots, cut into ½-inch chunks

2 stalks celery, cut into ½-inch chunks

1 leek, white and light green parts only, washed and cut into ½-inch chunks

3 sprigs parsley, with stems

3 sprigs thyme

1 large bay leaf

6 whole black peppercorns

Veal Stock

4 pounds veal knuckle bones

1 tablespoon tomato paste (for brown veal stock only)

1 large leek, cut into 1-inch pieces

1 cup coarsely chopped onions

¾ cup coarsely chopped carrots

¾ cup coarsely chopped celery

4 stems parsley

2 sprigs fresh thyme

1 bay leaf (not California)

1 teaspoon black peppercorns

ou can make the veal stock either white or brown, depending on the kind of recipe that requires it.

FOR WHITE VEAL STOCK

Place bones in stockpot and pour in enough cold water to cover by 2 inches. Bring to a boil, uncovered, over medium-high heat. Reduce heat to very low and simmer very gently, with just a few bubbles at the edges, for 5 hours.

Add remaining ingredients to bones in the stockpot and continue to simmer for 1 to 2 more hours. Turn off heat and let stock cool down, uncovered, for 1 hour.

FOR BROWN VEAL STOCK

Preheat oven to 400°F. Arrange veal bones in a single layer in an oiled large roasting pan. Roast, uncovered, for 30 minutes. Brush bones with tomato paste and continue to roast 30 minutes longer, or until bones are golden brown on all sides. Leave oven on.

Transfer bones to a large stockpot and pour in enough cold water to cover by 2 inches. Bring to a boil, uncovered, over medium-high heat. Reduce heat to very low and simmer very gently, with just a few bubbles at the edges, for 5 hours.

Meanwhile, spread leek, onions, carrots, and celery in a single layer in roasting pan that held bones, tossing vegetables with any fats from bones. Roast, uncovered, for 20 minutes, or until vegetables are golden brown. Transfer vegetables to a bowl. Add ½ cup water to hot roasting pan, stirring and scraping up brown bits, then add to stockpot.

Add browned vegetables and remaining ingredients to bones in stockpot and continue to simmer for 1 to 2 more hours. Turn off heat and let stock cool down, uncovered, for 1 hour.

FOR BOTH STOCKS

Using tongs or a slotted spoon, carefully remove bones from stock and discard them. Line a fine sieve with several layers of cheesecloth. Using a ladle, carefully strain stock through the sieve into a clean metal container.

If not using stock immediately, place metal container in a cold ice water bath. Stir liquid regularly as it cools down. As stock cools, it may be necessary to add more ice to the bath. The entire batch must be cooled down to 40°F.

Portion stock into containers and store them, covered, in the refrigerator for up to 7 days or in the freezer for up to 6 months. Skim fat from surface and bring to a full boil before using.

Venison Stock

M ake friends with a hunter to get your hands on some venison bones, or else call ahead at the butcher shop and put in a request.

YIELD: 8 CUPS

3 pounds venison bones, trimmings, and meat scraps

¼ cup tomato paste

4 quarts water

1 large onion, peeled and cut into chunks

1 large carrot, peeled and cut into ½-inch chunks

2 stalks celery, including leaves, cut into ½-inch chunks

3 sprigs parsley, with stems

3 sprigs thyme

1 large bay leaf

6 whole black peppercorns

6 juniper berries

¼ pound dried porcini mushrooms (optional)

Preheat oven to 400°F. Arrange venison bones in a single layer in an oiled large roasting pan. Roast, uncovered, for 30 minutes. Brush bones with tomato paste and continue to roast 30 minutes longer, or until bones are golden brown on all sides. Leave oven on.

Transfer bones to a large stockpot and add water. Bring to a boil, uncovered, over medium-high heat. Reduce heat to very low and simmer very gently, with just a few bubbles at the edges, for 5 hours.

Meanwhile, spread onion, carrot, and celery pieces in a single layer in roasting pan that held bones, tossing vegetables with any fats from bones. Roast, uncovered, for 20 minutes, or until vegetables are golden brown. Transfer vegetables to a bowl. Add ½ cup water to hot roasting pan, stirring and scraping up brown bits, then add to stockpot.

Add browned vegetables and remaining ingredients to bones in stockpot and continue to simmer for 1 to 2 more hours. Turn off heat and let the stock cool down, uncovered, for 1 hour.

Using tongs or a slotted spoon, carefully remove bones from stock and discard them. Line a fine sieve with several layers of cheesecloth. Using a ladle, carefully strain stock through the sieve into a clean metal container.

If not using immediately, place metal container in a cold ice water bath. Stir liquid regularly as it cools down. As stock cools, it may be necessary to add more ice to the bath. The entire batch must be cooled down to 40°F.

Portion stock into containers and store them, covered, in the refrigerator for up to 7 days or in the freezer for up to 6 months. Skim fat from surface and bring to a full boil before using.

CHAPTER 14

SANDWICHES & LATE-NIGHT SNACKS

On any given night any one of our ships feels like a major metropolitan city on a Saturday night: parts of our floating town are still well-lit and hopping, and other sections dark, housing those who want to get an early start in the morning. Like a glamorous city, there's always something to do after the shows let out, and generally it involves eating and drinking. Now the folks who had an early seating for dinner can be looking for something substantive, such as a Grilled Portobello Mushroom and Veggie Club Sandwich. Others, who've nibbled their way through the night, seek an adventurous grazing experience, including the likes of our world-famous *Bitterballen*—a croquette enjoyed by Dutch seafaring

GLACIER DROP

Sandra Scragg, manager beverage revenue and services

Ice blue and lemony, this Holland America Line signature cocktail comes complete with an ocean view.

2 wedges lemon, plus 1 extra for garnish

1½ ounces vodka

¼ ounce blue curaçao

1½ ounces homemade sour mix (see Pantry Staples)

Sugar, for garnish

In a pint glass, hand-press 2 lemon wedges with a muddler. Fill glass with ice. Add vodka, blue curaçao, and sour mix. Cap with shaker can and shake vigorously. Strain into a chilled martini glass with a sugared half rim. Garnish with remaining lemon wedge.

YIELD: 1 DRINK

CHRISTIAN CARBILLET
Executive chef

Many people forgo mayonnaise and prefer to spread sandwiches with butter, but there's no reason to settle for just plain butter. Try this delicious old recipe: Mix 1 stick butter with a heaping teaspoon of curry powder and 1 teaspoon lemon juice. Add salt to taste. Use as a spread for cooked sliced chicken or turkey sandwiches, filled with watercress or baby spinach. Add mango chutney to the sandwich, if desired.

men of the past—or our signature Coconut Shrimp with Thai Peanut Sauce and Spicy Pineapple Chutney.

Our eclectic late-night menu—including canapés, small tartlets, and other waiter-passed delicacies—could provide recipes for a whole cookbook. The selections here are versatile, great for any time of day, whether on a brunch table, as appetizers, as the centerpiece of a buffet, or even for a lunch box.

Below the bright lights and big-city feeling of Holland America Line's fabulous late nightlife, the lights are shining down on the stainless steel in our galleys and the kitchen crew. As our late-night revelers ponder what morsels will help them have sweet dreams, at least ten chefs and bakers are burning the midnight oil preparing for the meals that will greet our early risers . . . and so the cycle on board our ships begins again.

Grilled Portobello Mushroom and Veggie Club Sandwich

Though the exact late-nineteenth-century origin of the club sandwich is obscure, two things are certain: it's an American invention and the components of toast, meat, and salad seem to be the starting point. (A third layer of toast is often used, but that was a much later addition and remains a contentious issue among sandwich lovers.) Here, the finest meat substitute known on earth—grilled portobellos—stands in for the traditional chicken or turkey.

Prepare grill (medium heat). Brush both sides of portobello mushrooms with oil. Place on grill rack and grill on both sides until tender, about 20 minutes. Let cool slightly and then cut into ¼-inch-wide strips. Season with salt and pepper. (Alternatively, roast mushrooms on a rimmed baking sheet for 15 minutes at 400°F.)

In a bowl, blend mayonnaise, mustard, lemon juice, and cayenne. Season with salt and black pepper.

Lay 3 slices toast on a work surface and spread them with mayonnaise mixture. Top with sprouts, cucumber, and arugula. Top with slices of avocado and portobello. Sprinkle grated Gruyère on the mushrooms and top with tomato slices. Spread remaining 3 toast slices with mayonnaise mixture and place them on sandwiches. Cut in half and serve.

YIELD: 3 SANDWICHES

2 medium portobello mushroom caps

3 tablespoons olive oil

Salt

Freshly ground black pepper

½ cup mayonnaise

2 tablespoons Dijon mustard

2 tablespoons fresh lemon juice

⅛ teaspoon cayenne pepper

6 slices bread (whole grain or other), lightly toasted

1 cup packed alfalfa sprouts

1 small European (seedless) cucumber, very thinly sliced crosswise

½ cup packed arugula leaves

1 avocado, peeled, pitted, and sliced ¼-inch thick

½ cup grated Gruyère cheese

1 red tomato, thinly sliced

1 yellow tomato, thinly sliced

Prosciutto and Cheese Panini with Pesto Mayonnaise

YIELD: 2 SANDWICHES

2 tablespoons mayonnaise

2 tablespoons pesto
(see Pantry Staples)

2 pieces flat focaccia bread,
4-inches square, or 4 slices
country-style bread

Extra virgin olive oil for brushing

1 cup mixed gourmet salad greens

¼ pound prosciutto, thinly sliced

¼ pound mozzarella or fontina
cheese, thinly sliced

Munch these crispy snack sandwiches anytime during the day or evening. They're versatile, so add what you like, including chopped roasted red bell peppers, arugula, or thinly sliced tomato and garlicky balsamic dressing instead of mayonnaise.

In a small bowl, whisk together mayonnaise and pesto until blended.

Preheat an electric panini press.

For each sandwich, cut 1 focaccia square in half horizontally. Lightly brush the outer side of each slice with olive oil. Flip 1 slice over and spread with pesto mayonnaise. Top with greens and then with prosciutto and cheese. Position the other focaccia slice on the top, oiled side up. Repeat procedure with remaining ingredients to make other sandwich.

Arrange sandwiches in the panini press. Place press on sandwiches and cook until grill marks appear, about 1 to 2 minutes. Transfer sandwiches to a cutting board and cut in half. Serve immediately with additional pesto mayonnaise on the side.

NOTE

An electric panini press is not required for this recipe. Cook the sandwiches on a ridged stovetop grill pan over medium-high heat, weighing them down with a press, heavy saucepan, or a foil-covered brick after you've flipped them. Or cook sandwiches in a double-sided electric grill (hold the top down for the first few minutes of cooking). Panini made with sturdy bread such as focaccia or ciabatta can be put on a gas or charcoal grill over medium heat. If none of these options are possible, just wrap them in foil and bake them at 400°F for ½ hour, pressing down on them about halfway through cooking.

Cobb Salad Wrap

This wrap is the perfect kit bag for Cobb Salad, which would have a hard time staying together in any other kind of sandwich. Enjoy this at home, at the office, or furtively slumped in a seat at the movies while you wait for the show to start.

Preheat grill (medium-high heat) or broiler. Season chicken with salt and pepper. Grill or broil chicken until just cooked through, about 4 minutes per side. Let cool and slice into ¼-inch strips.

TO ASSEMBLE
Warm tortillas until pliable according to the package instructions. Lay chicken strips on the half of tortilla closest to you. Top with bacon, tomato, avocado, lettuce, and onion. Drizzle with blue cheese dressing. Tightly roll up tortillas, tucking in sides on first roll, and then finish rolling. Cut in half diagonally and serve.

> **TIP** | For a more "bready" experience when eating wrap sandwiches, substitute lavash, the Armenian cracker bread, for the flour tortillas. Lavash is available in 2 forms: soft pliable rounds and crisp rectangular crackers, and can be found in Middle Eastern markets or in the bread section of most supermarkets. Use soft lavash as is, folding in the sides as you roll to enclose the filling completely. To make crisp lavash pliable, rinse it under cold water and place it on the counter between 2 damp, clean kitchen towels for 45 minutes. (This technique has been used for centuries to freshen this flatbread, which is prized for its keeping qualities.) If the lavash begins to crack or split as you roll the sandwich, mist it lightly with water (a plant mister works well) or cover it with a damp dish towel for 15 minutes before continuing. —**Franz Schaunig**, executive chef

---

YIELD: 1 WRAP SANDWICH

1 half skinless boneless chicken breast

Salt

Freshly ground black pepper

1 extra-large flour tortilla, flavored if desired (with tomato or pesto, for example)

2 strips crisply cooked thick-slab bacon

½ tomato, seeded and diced

½ avocado, peeled, pitted, and thinly sliced

1 large leaf romaine lettuce, chopped

1 large leaf iceberg lettuce, chopped

4 thin slices red onion

2 tablespoons chunky blue cheese dressing

Coconut Shrimp with Thai Peanut Sauce and Spicy Pineapple Chutney

YIELD: 3–4 SERVINGS

SPICY PINEAPPLE CHUTNEY

4 ripe tomatoes, seeded and diced small

1 ripe pineapple, peeled, cored, and diced small

1 large red onion, peeled and diced small

2 scallions, white and tender green portions only, chopped

½ cup cilantro leaves, finely chopped

2 tablespoons fresh lemon juice

2 tablespoons white wine vinegar

1 teaspoon finely minced fresh ginger

½ teaspoon finely minced jalapeño pepper

½ teaspoon crushed red pepper

2 tablespoons sugar

Salt

Freshly ground black pepper

¼ cup extra virgin olive oil

PEANUT SAUCE

¾ cup smooth peanut butter, preferably unsweetened

¼ cup low-sodium soy sauce

2 tablespoons light brown sugar (omit if peanut butter is sweetened)

Juice of 2 limes

2 teaspoons minced fresh ginger

1 clove garlic, minced

Asian chili sauce (such as sambal; see Notes)

½ cup hot water

2 tablespoons minced cilantro (optional)

¼ cup chopped peanuts (optional), for garnish

esides being a cozy snack to share with someone very special, these crunchy shrimp are superlative party food: One hand brings them from dip to mouth while the other holds your piña colada (though a crisp sparkling wine would do nicely, too).

FOR THE SPICY PINEAPPLE CHUTNEY

In a nonreactive bowl, combine the first 10 ingredients (tomatoes through crushed red pepper). Stir in sugar. Season with salt and pepper. Set aside for 1 hour to blend flavors. Stir in oil.

FOR THE PEANUT SAUCE

In a food processor or blender, combine peanut butter, soy sauce, brown sugar (if using), lime juice, ginger, and garlic. Purée to combine. Season with chili sauce. While the motor is running, drizzle in hot water to thin out sauce—you may not need all of it. Pour sauce into a serving bowl. Fold in cilantro (if using). Garnish with chopped peanuts (if using). Refrigerate until needed. (Bring sauce to room temperature before serving with coconut shrimp.)

FOR THE COCONUT SHRIMP

Peel and devein shrimp, keeping tails intact. (You may also butterfly shrimp, if you wish.) In a shallow bowl, mix together flour, salt, white pepper, and cayenne. In another shallow bowl, whisk together eggs and cream. In a pie pan, combine coconut and bread crumbs.

Dredge shrimp in flour mixture and shake off excess. Working in batches, dip shrimp thoroughly in egg mixture and then press them into coconut mixture; turn shrimp over and press into coconut again to get full coverage. (Try to keep 1 hand dry, which makes the procedure less messy.) Lay out shrimp so they do not touch on a parchment-lined baking sheet or platter until ready to fry.

Add enough of the oil to a Dutch oven, heavy skillet, or deep fryer to measure 1½ inches deep. Attach deep-fry thermometer to side of pan (do not allow tip to touch bottom of pan). Heat oil to 350°F.

Gently submerge 4 shrimp in oil and deep-fry until coconut is golden brown, about 3 minutes. Using tongs or a slotted spoon, transfer shrimp to paper towels to drain. Repeat with remaining shrimp in batches of 4. Serve hot or at room temperature with dipping sauces.

NOTES

- Asian chili sauce is available at Indian and Southeast Asian markets and in the ethnic foods section of many supermarkets.

- For a flavor twist, add 3 tablespoons curry powder to the flour mixture for the shrimp.

- The chutney is also delicious with ham, pork chops, duck breast, or grilled tuna or swordfish. For a simpler alternative, try this pineapple marmalade dipping sauce: In a nonreactive saucepan over low heat, combine 2 cups chopped pineapple, 1 cup sugar, 1 cup white wine, and ⅛ teaspoon crushed red pepper. Barely simmer for 5 minutes. Set aside for 30 minutes to cool. (Store, covered, in the refrigerator for up to 2 days.) Rewarm slightly just before serving.

COCONUT SHRIMP

18 uncooked large shrimp (about 1 pound)

½ cup flour (see Notes)

¼ teaspoon kosher salt

¼ teaspoon freshly ground white pepper

¼ teaspoon cayenne pepper

3 eggs

⅓ cup heavy cream

1¼ cups sweetened shredded coconut

1¼ cups plain bread crumbs

6 cups peanut oil or canola oil

Thai Chicken Wrap

W raps travel well, handle well, and with good-quality ingredients taste amazing! Perfect for lunch, these flavorful wraps make terrific dinner options, too.

FOR THE MANGO SALSA AND THAI BARBECUE SAUCE

In a nonreactive bowl, combine all mango salsa ingredients except for pepper sauce, salt, and pepper; mix thoroughly. Add chipotle sauce (or hot pepper sauce) to taste. Season with salt and pepper. In a second bowl, thoroughly whisk all Thai barbecue sauce ingredients except for pepper sauce. Add chipotle pepper sauce (or hot pepper sauce) to taste.

FOR THE CHICKEN WRAP

Preheat grill (medium-high heat) or broiler. Season chicken with salt and pepper. Grill or broil chicken until just cooked through, about 4 minutes per side. Let cool and coarsely chop.

In a skillet, heat butter over medium-high heat. Add spinach and sauté for 1 minute; remove from heat and set aside.

TO ASSEMBLE

Warm tortillas until pliable according to the package instructions. Divide chicken and spinach between tortillas, placing them on the half of the tortilla closest to you. For each wrap, top chicken and spinach with ½ cup rice, ¼ cup beans, and ¼ cup mango salsa. Drizzle with Thai barbecue sauce to taste. Tightly roll up tortillas, tucking in sides on first roll, and then finish rolling. Cut in half diagonally and serve with sour cream and more salsa and Thai and regular barbecue sauce.

> TIP To incorporate crunch without moisture to sandwiches, add alfalfa or sunflower sprouts. If you want to grow your own sprouts, you can do it in 5 to 10 days (and you don't need dirt). There are several sources on the Internet to instruct you step by step. —**Martin Groenendyk**, executive chef

---

YIELD: 2 WRAP SANDWICHES

MANGO SALSA

1 mango, peeled, pitted, and diced

2 jalapeño peppers, minced

Juice of 2 limes

½ red bell pepper, diced

½ red onion, diced

2 tablespoons olive oil

¼ cup cilantro leaves, coarsely chopped

Chipotle pepper sauce or hot pepper sauce

Salt

Freshly ground black pepper

THAI BARBECUE SAUCE

¼ cup peanut butter

¼ cup barbecue sauce

2 tablespoons soy sauce

Chipotle sauce or hot pepper sauce

CHICKEN WRAP

1 whole skinless boneless chicken breast

Salt

Freshly ground black pepper

½ tablespoon unsalted butter

1 large handful fresh spinach, washed well and dried

2 extra-large flour tortillas, flavored if desired (with tomato or pesto, for example)

1 cup cooked jasmine rice flavored with turmeric, cumin, and chili powder in equal amounts

½ cup black beans

Sour cream

Bitterballen with Mustard

4 tablespoons unsalted butter

½ pound beef or veal (even pot roast), chopped fine but not ground

¼ cup finely diced carrots

½ cup finely chopped onion

Salt

Freshly ground black pepper

Pinch freshly grated nutmeg

1 tablespoon fresh lemon juice

2 tablespoons finely chopped parsley

5 tablespoons flour, plus ½ cup extra for rolling

1 cup beef stock (see Pantry Staples) or milk

½ cup panko (see Note, page 48) or dried bread crumbs

1 egg, beaten with 1 teaspoon water

Vegetable oil, for deep frying

Deep-fried parsley, for garnish

Mustard, for dipping

These Dutch beef croquettes, served at parties and other festive occasions, consist of small balls of meat, butter, bouillon, flour, and herbs that are breaded and deep fried. Flavorings abound: one manufacturer features twenty-eight different herb combinations. In the Netherlands, *bitterballen* are typically served with mustard for dipping, but your pantry's the limit when it comes to the dips, chutneys, and barbecue sauces that can complement these crispy, creamy morsels.

In a large skillet, heat 1 tablespoon butter over medium heat. Add beef, carrots, and onion. Cook, stirring, until meat is browned and carrots are tender. Briefly drain meat mixture in a colander and transfer to a mixing bowl. Season with salt, pepper, and nutmeg. Stir in lemon juice and parsley. Set aside.

In a medium saucepan, heat the remaining 3 tablespoons butter over medium heat. Add 5 tablespoons flour and cook, stirring well, for 2 to 3 minutes. Add beef stock or milk. Continue cooking, stirring constantly, until thick. Scrape flour mixture into meat mixture and stir to combine thoroughly. Cover and refrigerate for at least 2 hours, or until completely cold and solidified.

With your hands, roll meat mixture into 1-inch balls. In a shallow bowl, mix together remaining ½ cup flour, ¼ teaspoon salt, and ¼ teaspoon pepper. Place panko (or bread crumbs) in another shallow bowl. In a third bowl, whisk egg and water mixture.

With your hands, roll balls in seasoned flour, then in the egg mixture, then in panko, and then back into the egg mixture, and then lastly in panko again. Lay out *bitterballen* so they do not touch on a parchment-lined baking sheet or platter until ready to fry.

Add enough oil to a Dutch oven, heavy skillet, or deep fryer to measure at least 2 inches deep. Attach deep-fry thermometer to side of pan (do not allow tip to touch bottom of pan). Heat oil to 375°F.

Add a few *bitterballen* at a time to oil and deep-fry until golden brown, about 2 to 3 minutes. Using tongs or a slotted spoon, transfer *bitterballen* to paper towels to drain. Repeat with remaining *bitterballen* in batches. Serve hot or at room temperature with deep-fried parsley and mustard, or whatever dipping sauce you prefer.

WHAT'S COOKING:

Holland America Line's new Culinary Arts Center offers a state-of-the-art kitchen where our master chefs and celebrity guest chefs demonstrate their arts.

OUR OVERARCHING MISSION IS TO MAKE EACH HOLLAND America Line experience the most memorable and rewarding journey of our guests' lives. To that end, we provide a seamless experience in which our guests can make the most of our facilities, our programming, and our itineraries; for example, the dining experience aboard our ships reflects the customs and cuisines of our ports of call; our onboard events and programming include enrichment activities that help our guests embrace and appreciate the cuisine and culture that greets them when they disembark at a given destination.

Over our long history as a company, there have been countless subtle evolutions and many great revolutions in creating this seamless experience between ship and shore for our guests. Most recently, we've taken a quantum leap: the development and opening of our onboard Culinary Arts Centers—state-of-the-art "show kitchens at sea," where guests can learn new cooking techniques and dishes. Furthermore, Holland America Line has partnered with *Food & Wine* magazine to provide guests on select Holland America Line cruises an opportunity to experience demonstrations and seminars conducted by top chefs, wine experts, and leading cookbook authors. In our Culinary Arts centers, our guests can learn tricks of the trade from the most celebrated names in the professional food world and are able to try their hand at preparing dishes and tasting wines representative of specific ports of call. Another programming aspect of our "Signature of Excellence" culinary program is that each year the Culinary Arts Center features additional culinary demonstrations by regional and specialty chefs from ports visited including Mexico, Alaska, Europe, and Asia/Pacific cruises. Members of our own talented culinary arts team, including our Consulting Master Chef Rudi Sodamin, conduct lectures, demonstrations and hands-on cooking classes on every sailing of every ship.

At Holland America Line, we have received myriad accolades and honors, including "Best Overall Cruise Value" for many consecutive years

THE BIG PICTURE

by the prestigious World Ocean & Cruise Liner Society, as well as being one of the higest-rated cruise lines year after year as voted on by the readers of *Travel + Leisure* magazine. But the greatest honor and privilege the entire Holland America Line team has, and the most rewarding part of what we do, is knowing that we have provided our guests with unique opportunities and experiences. The stellar chefs celebrated in the pages of *Food & Wine* magazine, our own culinary team, and our Culinary Arts Center and dining areas eagerly await your next visit—your next adventure in cooking, dining, and premium travel to the world's greatest destinations.

RICK MEADOWS

CTC, Holland America Line, Senior Vice President, Marketing & Sales

Rick Meadows (center) is joined by a group of celebrity chefs to announce our partnership with *Food & Wine* magazine.

CONVERSION TABLES

WEIGHTS

AMERICAN	METRIC
⅛ ounce	3.5 grams
¼ ounce	7 ½–8 grams
½ ounce	15 grams
¾ ounce	20 grams
1 ounce	30 grams
2 ounces	55 grams
3 ounces	85 grams
4 ounces (¼ pound)	110 grams
5 ounces	140 grams
6 ounces	170 grams
7 ounces	200 grams
8 ounces (½ pound)	225 grams
9 ounces	255 grams
10 ounces	285 grams
11 ounces	310 grams
12 ounces (¾ pound)	340 grams
13 ounces	370 grams
14 ounces	400 grams
15 ounces	425 grams
16 ounces (1 pound)	450 grams
1¼ pounds	560 grams
1½ pounds	675 grams
2 pounds	900 grams
3 pounds	1.35 kilos
4 pounds	1.8 kilos
5 pounds	2.3 kilos
6 pounds	2.7 kilos
7 pounds	3.2 kilos
8 pounds	3.4 kilos
9 pounds	4.0 kilos
10 pounds	4.5 kilos

TEMPERATURES

FAHRENHEIT	CELSIUS	GAS MARK
40	4.45	
50	10	
65	18.3	
105	40.5	
115	46	
120	49	
125	51.65	
130	54.4	
135	57.25	
150	70	
175	80	
200	100	0
225	110	¼
250	130	½
275	140	1
300	150	2
325	170	3
350	180	4
375	190	5
400	200	6
425	220	7
450	230	8
475	240	9
500	250	
525	270	
550	290	

LIQUID MEASURES

	FLUID OUNCES	MILLILITER
¼ cup	3	60
⅓ cup	4	80
½ cup	6¼	120
1 cup	12.5	240
1 pint (2 cups)	20	570
¾ pint	15	425
½ pint	10	290
⅓ pint	6.6	190
¼ pint	5	150
1 quart	50	960
1 gallon	200	3.84 liters
2 scant tablespoons	1	28
1 tablespoon	½	15
1 teaspoon	–	5
½ teaspoon	–	2.5
¼ teaspoon	–	1.25

LENGTHS

AMERICAN	METRIC
¼ inch	6 millimeters
½ inch	12 millimeters
1 inch	2½ centimeters
2 inches	5 centimeters
4 inches	10 centimeters
6 inches	15 centimeters
8 inches	20 centimeters
10 inches	25 centimeters
12 inches	30 centimeters
14 inches	35 centimeters
16 inches	40 centimeters
18 inches	45 centimeters

APPROXIMATE AMERICAN/METRIC CONVERSIONS

ITEM	USA	METRIC
Flour	1 cup / 4¼ ounces	115 grams
Granulated sugar	1 cup / 7 ounces	200 grams
Brown sugar (packed)	1 cup / 8 ounces	225 grams
Brown sugar (packed)	1 tablespoon / ½ ounce	15 grams
Butter	1 cup / 8 ounces	225 grams
Raisins (loose)	1 cup / 5¼ ounces	145 grams
Uncooked rice	1 cup / 7 ounces	200 grams
Cocoa powder	¼ cup / ¾ ounce	20 grams

ACKNOWLEDGMENTS

No memorable meal was ever made from a single ingredient. No cruise ship could ever pull out of port with a crew of one. And no cookbook worth its salt was ever a solitary undertaking.

Without the creative and executive support of Johan Groothuizen, vice president, marine hotel operations, who brought me aboard Holland America Line as master chef culinary consultant, I could not have brought this collection of exciting recipes to you. Johan is one of those bold executives who embraces evolution, who appreciates artistry, and who understands that no quest for excellence was ever realized without sailing bravely into uncharted waters.

Kudos and thanks to all the members of the Holland America Line culinary department, including Steve Kirsch, director of culinary operation; Jafar Al-Shibibi, corporate manager of guest and dining services; and John Peijs, manager marine hotel operations onboard systems, for their insight and input into this project and for their commitment to the care of each and every Holland America Line guest. I'd like to extend a special thanks as well to Guenther Cussigh, corporate executive chef, who puts his heart into the Holland America Line culinary experience and is an inspiration to his corporate culinary trainers John Mulvaney and Guido Scarpellino, and Michel Berhocoirigoin, corporate executive pastry chef; to the rest of the truly talented culinary team; and to Sandra Scragg, who leads the corporate beverage team.

The book you hold in your hands also exists because of the commitment, enthusiastic support, and genius of a handful of remarkable people, each of whom understands with a unique and unwavering vision what makes Holland America Line a brand of distinction, elegance, and incomparable excellence: Stein Kruse, president and chief executive officer; Rick Meadows, senior vice president, marketing and sales; Dan Grausz, senior vice president, fleet operations; Judy Palmer, vice president, marketing communications; and the tireless Rose Abello, vice president, public relations.

Like any great meal, a book is not just the sum of its contents, but it is the product of carefully tended and beautifully presented ingredients. To me, *Holland America Line A Taste of Excellence* is not just a collection of recipes, but a *chef-d'oeuvre* thanks to the contributions of a diverse group of artists with whom I am honored to work: photographers Herb Schmitz and Pat Doyle, whose pictures not only reflect their skill, but their souls; my wordsmiths Marcelle Langan DiFalco and Monica Velgos, who capture not only the essentials but the essence of my culinary passions and predilections. Furthermore, I am deeply grateful to Rizzoli Publishing for counting me among its stable of illustrious authors; no publisher on the planet puts forth such intelligent and beautifully rendered cookbooks. Special thanks too to my editor Tricia Levi and the Rizzoli design team for their contributions to this book and making it the beautiful volume that it is.

And, like a sumptuous dessert, I save the best for last. To my wonderful wife Bente, my most cherished beloved, to my fine sons Magnus and Kenneth, and to my lovely daughter Kristina, you are all the sweetness of my life.

RUDI SODAMIN
Master Chef, Culinary Consultant, Holland America Line

INDEX

A TASTE OF EXCELLENCE

A behind-the-scenes look at chefs in the galley.